Praise for *Healing*

"Alicia King is no stranger to the disorienting pain of losing people she loves—and that empathy informs a concise, clear how-to book for anyone trying to help someone else cope with a major loss. Practical in both adaptability suggestions and insight into the varying forms of grief, *[Healing]* will increase comfort and even more importantly, greatly reduce missteps, faux pas, and the awkward feeling of not knowing what to do."

—*Holly Gleason,*
The Yummy List

"Alicia King has written a profoundly insightful and much-needed book for our society. I found it to be thorough, gentle, and yes, at times surprising! Wonder no more. *[Healing]* fills in all the blanks."

—*Lynn Foster,*
Steering Committee Member, The Compassionate Friends

Healing

Healing

The Essential Guide to Helping Others Overcome Grief & Loss

Alicia King

TURNER

Turner Publishing Company

445 Park Avenue, 9th Floor
New York, NY 10022

200 4th Avenue North, Suite 950
Nashville, TN 37219

Healing: The Essential Guide to Helping Others Overcome Grief and Loss

www.turnerpublishing.com

Cover design by Mike Penticost

Library of Congress Cataloging-in-Publication Data

King, Alicia.
 Healing : the essential guide to helping others overcome grief and loss / Alicia King.
    p. cm.
 ISBN 978-1-59652-816-1
1. Grief. 2. Loss (Psychology) 3. Healing. 4. Bereavement--Psychological aspects. I. Title.
 BF575.G7K529 2011
 155.9'3--dc22

2011000479

Printed in the United States of America

11 12 13 14 15 16 17 18 — 0 9 8 7 6 5 4 3 2 1

This book is also available in gift book format as
Sorry For Your Loss: What People Who Are Grieving Wish You Knew
(978-1-59652-747-8).

For my husband, Dan, who will find the truth and the humor in any situation. You're my compass. Thank you for believing we can do anything.

For Faith Carol, who was named perfectly. My pragmatic little baby-whisperer. I'm keeping the card.

For David, my blog editor, comic relief, and wunderkind. Your encouragement is a gift. Now, hurry!

For my parents, Jon and Carol, for a million reasons. I am who I am because of who you were.

To everyone who shared their story with me. May those you love never be forgotten.

Grief knits two hearts in closer bonds than happiness ever can; and common sufferings are far stronger links than common joys.

—ALPHONSE DE LAMARTINE

A real friend is one who walks in when the rest of the world walks out.

—WALTER WINCHELL

Contents

Introduction

It all started when my mom died. It wasn't exactly your average death, if that even exists. For starters, she was 48. She was also very smart, pretty, and funny as hell. One last thing—her death was investigated as a homicide. Her boyfriend was the suspect.

I told you it wasn't average.

It was on the news, the front page, and every gossip's tongue. You'd think I would have been surrounded by people wanting to talk, and to help, right? Not exactly. Many did, of course, but many more were simply too freaked out by the whole mess. They acted like they didn't know. They said the worst thing possible: nothing.

I wondered why these normally warm and caring people would act this way. Wonderful people. Friends since elementary school. People I knew well and loved dearly. Silent. Their distance made what was already a nightmare even worse. Eventually, I chalked it up to the strange circumstances and slowly went on with my life.

Ten years later my father died in his sleep. It was totally unexpected. My parents died very differently, so why were people's reactions so similar? While many were kind and loving, many more seemed painfully uncomfortable in my presence. Why?

I know they wanted to reach out to me, comfort me, and help me through it. They simply didn't know how. But how can that be? Everyone dies. It is said that for every person who dies, hundreds mourn. How can we not know what to do?

After each death I looked for a book about other people's experiences surrounding the loss of a family member, but I never found what I needed. I found dated pamphlets. I found books for dealing with grief specific to widowhood, loss of a pet, and divorce. They felt cold and clinical. I didn't want a how-to manual as much as an honest peek into the grief of others. Was it like mine? Were they doing the same things and feeling the same way? How did people react to them? Was my family normal? Was I crazy?

Would I be okay?

It seems like a form of cruelty to have to guess what someone needs while grieving when the simple remedy is to share what we've learned. It's that easy. If everyone who is surviving grief would honestly discuss the experience, just imagine the impact! Share what helped and what didn't. Talk about what you needed and what you didn't. Tell others what you now do for others who are grieving. Discuss what you wish those around you had known.

I want to show you what it's really like for someone after a death. Not the happy public face we often put on. One woman I interviewed called it her "fake fine." After her mother died, she pretended right away to be all right, just to end up feeling bitter later about the lack of support she received. When I asked her why she did that, she explained that many of those around her were uncomfortable talking about it after a couple of weeks. She began to refuse help and insisted she was doing well. She put that "fake fine" on like armor every time she left the house. No wonder her co-workers thought she was okay. No wonder they stopped asking what they could do for her.

No wonder we don't understand the depths of grief until we're experiencing it ourselves.

Believe me, I know it can be hard to go to someone after a death. I have made nearly every mistake described in this book, but I'd rather risk making one of those mistakes again than ignore the person who is mourning. I've learned silence only deepens pain.

If you can't face going to their house for a visit, that's

okay. Go the service and give them a hug instead. Do you faint at funerals? Don't worry, you get a pass. Just give them a call. Are you afraid you won't know what to say on the phone? No problem, send a card.

Just do something. Anything.

This book is full of ideas. I'll keep giving you options until one feels right. They won't just be examples of what works, though. Oh no, I'll tell you ways it all went wrong, too. Good intentions don't always equal a good result. Sometimes they equal hilarious.

If you need immediate suggestions of how to help, go to the list at the end. That will get you started until you can finish the book.

That's the idea here. I want you to have everything you need to support someone as they grieve. I'll tell you what worked for others, what to expect, and mistakes you'll thank God you didn't make!

1

Listen. Then Listen Some More

1

Listen. Then Listen Some More

When I ask people who are grieving what comforts them, nearly every single person gives the same answer. "Someone to listen."

The same three words, over and over and over again. Someone to listen. The simplicity of this is important. They don't want someone to "fix" it. They're not asking for answers, spiritual wisdom, or uplifting cliches. Nope, they just need you to be there.

Don't doubt your ability to help the person who is grieving. What is needed most is something we all can do—show up. You don't need any special skills or education to be present.

Even professional bereavement counselors acknowledge this. The New York State Mental Health Office writes, "We are not the experts on anyone's grief. As bereavement workers we must meet the grieving without expectations about what should happen or what they should be feeling. There are no experts in this work."

Jan Davies is a Certified Whole Health Educator, with more than twenty years' experience as a hospice volunteer. She explains the importance of what she calls deep listening:

> The greatest gift we can give to another is our complete attention, which requires few words. Not just our mental attention but our intuitive attention as well, noticing body language, facial expressions, tears, sighs, and silence just as if they too are words. Oftentimes when people ask us what to do next, they're not really asking for our advice, but rather to be a witness to their own processes. Let go of the desire to fix the other person, or the need to make them feel better. Let go of the need to provide snazzy advice. All that inner attention robs the griever of your full attention. Deep listening replaces the fear of "don't know what to say" syndrome. We can "just listen" until something comes to us from our inner source of wisdom. Just be present. Be a witness. Be the calm in the storm. Be willing to laugh when they need to laugh. Be willing to allow tears

when they need to cry. Open your heart to the experience in spite of the possible pain. By supporting the bereaved in these ways, we create sacred space for them to heal in their own way and in their own time.

A widow I met told me, "The loss of a loved one needs to be acknowledged and the grieving person given the opportunity to speak about the loss, if they want to. I found talking about my loss after my late husband died, was extremely helpful. The attitude that someone should get over it and not cry and be strong with a stiff upper lip is also not helpful. It is much more helpful to give the person time to cry and make them feel safe and secure in sharing their grief and pain."

Don't underestimate the value of sitting with someone. It provides a comfort that most people deeply need after a death. At a time when loneliness can be painfully intense, your visit may be the only possible source of peace.

Sarah Gutin Beaty remembers, "When I was in high school, my boyfriend was killed in a car-train accident. I think the best thing for me was when people would shut up and just be there. I wanted them to recognize that I was grieving but not tell me it was going to be okay."

JoAnne Funch writes in her book, *How to Support Anyone Grieving a Loss,* "You don't have to understand someone's loss, just continue to be supportive. This means keeping in contact with them for weeks and months after loss.

You don't have to fix the person grieving—just be there to listen and they will give you the signs or directly communicate what they need, and if they don't, just listen in a nonjudgmental way."

That's important advice. Too often, we overwhelm those who are grieving. Try to hold back and take your cues from them before expressing too much emotion.

John and Cynthia Colagross were married for forty-seven years before John died of cancer. Cynthia advises, "Do not be over-solicitous of the survivors. Some people said things like, 'Oh, oh, oh, I am so, so sorry!' with an attitude of complete emotional devastation. A hug is enough for me. Maybe, 'Sorry for your loss.' Just let the person who has lost their loved one talk about it, and if they cry? Let them! If you are close to them, hug them. No need for words. You can cry too. It's all right to talk about the person who has passed away. They may have died, but they were a big part of your life, my life. Memories are wonderful."

Susan Petrina sums it up with a biblical example. "The first thing I want to say is learn a lesson from the early chapters of the book of Job. When Job loses everything, some of his friends come and sit with him in his grief. What a comfort the presence of someone who cares for us in our times of difficulty can be. Physical presence or sending cards or notes with simple offerings such as we're sorry, we're thinking of you, we're praying for you, is there anything we can do; these words can be a salve to the wound. Then his friends begin to speak . . . hmmmm, all of a sudden their presence isn't quite as comforting. The big lesson for us: being there for someone grieving is very good; trying to offer advice, or fill the space with words may not be helpful at all and may even be hurtful. Just let the person know you care and are thinking of them. Be available. Listen."

The Bottom Line: Go to them and listen. It's the simplest, yet most important thing you can do.

Resources

- *The Good Listener,* by James E. Sullivan
- *Listening: The Forgotten Skill: A Self-Teaching Guide,* by Madelyn Burley-Allen

Piglet sidled up to Pooh from behind. "Pooh" he whispered.

"Yes, Piglet?"

"Nothing," said Piglet, taking Pooh's paw. "I just wanted to be sure of you."

~A. A. Milne

Give sorrow words; the grief that does not speak whispers the o'er-fraught heart and bids it break.

~William Shakespeare

2

Give Them a Choice

2

Give Them a Choice

I have interviewed hundreds of people while writing this book, and most of them experienced difficulty making the simplest of decisions immediately following a death. It's ironic, right? Just when we need help more than ever, we are virtually incapable of knowing where to start when someone offers.

Time after time, people will tell the family in mourning, "Whatever you need, we're here for you. Just call us." This is sweet, but vague. When you can barely cope with getting out of bed, you may find managing your home, funeral arrangements and out-of-towners to be overwhelming. This is why so many people tell me they were grateful for concrete favors. When a neighbor asks, "Would you rather I bring dinner tonight or tomorrow?" this is easier to process than, "What do you need?" After all, what they really need is for this not to have happened.

There is no general favor that will fit every situation. If the person finds peace in being busy, then allow them to do that, then be there when they need to break down. For many, it's not the favors that are appreciated and remembered most. It's the hugs and permission to cry without judgment that got them through.

When Jerry and Susan's son, Spencer, died before his first birthday, they were given plenty of support. Sometimes too much. Susan explains:

Offer to help, offer again later, drop by a meal or two, offer to help clean the house, yard, pick up some groceries, whatever practical services you could do. Letting someone know you are available is the first step, then *listen* to what the person's needs are. I had people trying to help me in ways that were very painful. If they had just listened to me, we could have prevented some of the difficulties we experienced. Keep in mind the differences in personalities. Extroverts and introverts, we handle things differently. It isn't helpful when someone does something for me that I don't want done, or forces their help upon me when I don't need it. I accepted some help just because the person needed to do something for me so badly. I was essentially serving them. This goes two ways because the grieving person must be willing to accept help when they do need it, and express what kinds of things would be useful. I had some very helpful books passed on to me and one or two not so helpful ones. The great thing about books is that you can pick them up and read the whole thing or put them down. It is unintrusive (is that a word?). Do pass on a book that you think may help. Let them decide whether to read it or not. Anything you do for someone must be a freely offered gift with no expectations attached!

Susan's message is a great reminder. Ask yourself what they need, not what we think they need or what we want to give. Another thing to keep in mind is to offer only what we can deliver. Just before this book went to press, Susan and Jerry's youngest son, Andrew, also died of Spinal Muscular Atrophy, or SMA, the same disease Spencer had. Learn more at www.fightsma.org.

Angela has worked in hospice for more than twenty years. She told me about a man she met there named Jack. Jack's wife died after a car accident. Two days later he received a call from a couple they had known for many years. They offered their condolences and told him to ask them for whatever he needed. He thanked them and asked if they would mind going with him to the church the next day to plan the service. They told him they were sorry, but they had to work all day. He said he understood, then explained he had no one to take flowers home after the service on Saturday. Could they do that instead? They apologized and said they wouldn't be able to make the funeral. They were going out of town that day! The lesson here? Don't make a general offer of help. Keep it simple. Explain what you can do, then be sure and do it.

Sometimes the mundane can seem insurmountable. After a death, taking the garbage to the curb might feel like too much to handle, let alone mowing the lawn. Remember these tasks when reaching out. It all helps.

"I wish my friends had understood I wasn't dissolving into depression," says Rae Webber about the time following her mother's death. "I was just tired. So tired. Emotional exhaustion, I guess. I just needed to be sad. That meant nothing got done, though. I probably could have used a few more grocery deliveries and a few less offers of their Valiums!"

A young mom of three whose husband had just died remembers, "I grew to hate the call-me-no-matter-what-you-need-no-matter-what-time comment. I prefer, 'Do you need meals? Can I watch the kids after school?' I mean, if I need something at 3 a.m., I'll call my mom. If I don't know you that well, I'm not going to call you, so that means nothing. If you see they're overwhelmed, help them. The best was, 'I'm coming by Saturday to vacuum.' I was like, 'Thank you!' It was a basic thing, but I loved that."

Abigail Carter's husband, Arron, died in the Twin Towers on 9/11. She wrote the book *The Alchemy of Loss* as a testament to finding the silver lining of grief and loss, to discovering the defibrillator effect of trauma and its power to awaken us into really living. She says, "As for the don'ts, I am aware that every person handles grief differently and I tried to be understanding when some of the following happened to me."

I love Abigail's advice:

- Don't arrive at a bereaved person's door and burst into tears as you hug them. They will pat you on the back with a glazed look wishing they could help you through your grief, but they are not capable. Check your own grief at the door.
- Even if you would prefer to avoid the bereaved person indefinitely, even a "Sorry for your loss" (as much as we hate that line), is better than avoiding all eye contact.
- It's okay to talk about the loss with a bereaved person. In fact, they usually want to talk about their loved one.
- Making a bereaved person laugh will make their day.
- Offers of practical help, like babysitting or gift cards for massages, are most appreciated.

Abigail adds, "Early on, I most appreciated the people

who treated me the same as they always had, the ones that made me laugh and the ones who let me cry without getting freaked out. I also quite liked the ones who showed up with gelato on a Monday night without provocation."

Michele Neff-Hernandez explains how much small acts of kindness meant to her after her husband, Phil, died:

My next-door neighbor called every one of all three of my kids' teachers to let them know why they missed school the day after my husband died. She then sent me a note letting me know that she was driving my portion of our group carpool every day for an unlimited amount of time. I never asked, and didn't even know how badly I would need her generous assistance. She was like my own personal angel. One night I heard a commotion outside my front door. Two of my neighbors were standing outside of my car installing new windshield wiper blades. One of them noticed that I needed new ones, and they were trying to install them without bothering me!

Sometimes there's a need so obvious that you might assume someone else has taken care of it. Now's not the time to take chances. Don't ignore the elephant in the room. Ask! I love how John Lennon put it, "When you're drowning, you don't say 'I would be incredibly pleased if someone would have the foresight to notice me drowning and come and help me.' You just scream.'"

Don't wait for the scream. Jump in and help.

The Bottom Line: By all means, offer help, but don't make the griever guess. Be specific. Give options. Only offer what you can deliver.

Resources

- GriefShare is one of many support groups to consider. When the time is right, suggest they take a look: www.griefshare.org
- After the death of a child, Compassionate Friends can offer tremendous help to the family: www.compassionatefriends.org

It's the friends you can call up at 4 a.m. that matter.

~Marlene Dietrich

3

Beyond the Casserole: Food Ideas

3

Beyond the Casserole: Food Ideas

Cakes, cookies, pies, lasagnas, fried chicken, and the list goes on. We tend to bring these things to a family as soon as we hear about a death. They're called comfort foods for a reason.

Whatever chaos life gives us, we still have to eat. It's a constant need, and an easy way for us to show our love and concern.

People generally have lots of visitors in the days after a death, and house guests on top of that. They need to be fed. It's no wonder their refrigerators and counters soon fill up with the offerings of those who love them.

After their father died of pancreatic cancer, fifteen-year-old Jenny Siniard and her brother were alone in the house. She remembers, "The people who made a commitment to help really meant a lot to me, but some offers were superficial. People sent food over because they knew my brother and I had to get fed, but after a week, it just stopped. I guess they thought my dad had been magically resurrected, and was cooking for us again!"

This is a common situation, unfortunately. One week seems to be the cutoff for many families. After the funeral, the shock wears off and the crowd disappears. So does the food supply. You can help prevent this from happening.

Start a Dinner Calendar

There are several templates online I will list at the end of this chapter. Use one of them, or jot down your own on any calendar. Dinner calendars work well for many reasons:

- They regulate the flow of meals.
- They arrange more than just something to eat. They keep visitors coming during those too-quiet days or weeks following a death.
- They call for one person to manage the calendar, which makes it easier for the griever. If you are the manager, be sure and make reminder calls. I've yet

to meet the family for whom at least one dinner did not show up.

- They help communicate any personal needs or preferences with everyone. Post any food allergies and dislikes and best delivery times. Don't forget to change the number of people being served, as company comes and goes. Do they prefer a meal every other day? Is a deli tray better for weekends? This way the family has to tell only one person rather than repeat it over and over.
- They allow you to quickly post what each person has brought. This prevents a three-day run of chicken casseroles.
- They remind the cooks to bring only what can be eaten. Lots of leftovers are not only a nuisance, but can be a constant, painful reminder of the newly smaller family.

Encourage people to deliver food in disposable dishes, whenever possible. I'm as eco-minded as the next person, but let's agree to make grieving an exception. The washing and returning of dishes are not what the griever needs right now.

If you sign up for a night but your schedule won't allow you to prepare a meal, don't worry. Bring them take-out or have something delivered and meet them at the house.

Remember: your visit is half the gift.

Give Restaurant Gift Cards

This is another idea mentioned by family after family as one of the most appreciated gestures they received after a death. Find out which restaurants the family prefers, then share this with others who ask what they need. There will be many people wanting to help. They will appreciate knowing exactly what to do. It couldn't be easier, and it takes a load off the family caregiver's mind each night.

These cards are helpful for anyone, but especially for those with children at home.

I recently spoke to a father whose wife died nine months ago. He said he had just used his last gift card this month. He appreciated having them, especially when grandparents would stay with the kids overnight while he worked. It was less stressful for everyone to know that meals were covered. He felt better about asking for help, knowing they wouldn't have to cook. One last thing to worry about is always a good thing during times of great stress.

The Bottom Line: It can be a huge help to have food taken care of during a crisis. Organize your efforts so that assisting with meals helps even more.

Resources

- Here's a great site to make dinner calendars easy: http://takethemameal.com

Food is the most primitive form of comfort.

~Sheilah Graham

One of the very nicest things about life is the way we must regularly stop whatever it is we are doing and devote our attention to eating.

~Luciano Pavarotti

4

Gifts from a Group

4

Gifts from a Group

What do you do when you're not especially close to the person who is grieving, but you still want to do something for them? This may be someone from work, your neighborhood, church, or school.

Ask the person who knows them best for ideas. Would they appreciate maid service for a month? Gardening help? Could you send a card around to collect donations to the hospice, charity, or personal fund of their choice? This is often listed in the obituary. You'd be surprised how much they'll appreciate a line or two from each of you in a card.

Sending a group gift isn't permission to avoid the person. It's still important that you say something. It can be as simple as a hug and an "I'm so sorry." Send a card. Call. Send flowers. Anything is better than nothing.

Plant a Tree

After my father-in-law, Ray, passed away, a large group of our neighbors came by with a tree. They told my husband how they had enjoyed meeting Ray during his visits. They reached out to our whole family. They told us to pick out a place for the tree and they'd be back tomorrow to plant it. We then had a plaque made with Ray's name on it. This gift was so unexpected, and so thoughtful. It meant the world to my husband. It was good to hear them talk about Ray, and to know they were thinking of us during such a difficult time.

Donna Morris was nine months pregnant to the day when her son was stillborn. "What I really liked were the cards people sent. People got together and instead of sending money they planted trees in my child's name. For me, that was awesome. They sent notes saying they donated in Bryce's name, or they planted a tree for Bryce. Just people saying his name was so nice. It felt good to see his name in a card."

Funeral Features

You might consider putting something together for the funeral. Did the deceased have a favorite flower, song, or hobby? Incorporate that into a gesture for the family.

Maybe your group has pictures of the person who has died the family would enjoy seeing. A photo album or memory book would be a beautiful gift.

Dove Release

Consider arranging a dove release. This can be done after the church service, graveside during the burial, or even at their home after the services. Many people find this to be a beautiful way to symbolize letting go, saying goodbye, or even a soul's flight to heaven.

When Rodney Wilkinson's wife, Kathy, died, his friends wanted to do something special at her service. "The really cool thing that people got together to do that really honored Kathy was the dove release. I had never experienced something like that before. I didn't want a bunch of flowers at the house anyway, so for us, this was much better. It was great. It complemented what we had worked to put together that day. I didn't know about it until it was time, and it was a huge blessing. They had me lift the door and let them go. I'll never forget it."

Rodney's a great guy for being so flexible. In this case, it worked out well to arrange the dove release without his knowledge. Personally, I'd ask before springing such a surprise on someone at a funeral.

Is there a holiday coming up? This can be an opportunity to reach out, especially when there are children who are grieving.

Remember the Kids

A young mother remembers that first Christmas alone with her young children, just a few weeks after her husband died. "I heard a knock at the door on Christmas Eve. When I answered it, several professors from the university where my husband had worked were there. They had four big bags, full of gifts for my three children. It was wonderful."

Specifically for Them

Don't feel boxed-in as to what choices you have. There are as many ways to help as there are people. Does the person or family have any special hobbies or interests? Consider these things when deciding what to do.

My mom used to work in a commercial construction office with a woman named Judy. Judy was a talented painter. Several of her beautiful landscapes were featured in the office. When Judy's husband died, my mom got together with five other co-workers. They decided to buy some art supplies from her favorite store and take them to her, a bit at a time. This eased the tension each time they arrived. It gave them a place to start, and soon they were comfortable talking about Judy's husband, and how she was doing. She sent my mom several notes, thanking her for what she and the others had done. That was more than twenty years ago, but it made such an impression on me that I remember it well.

Walking Calendar

A great idea gaining popularity is a walking calendar. Here's how it works: a different person or family signs up to walk with the griever. The walks can be simple and short or full-blown hikes. They choose how often they need walking buddies and for how long. Whatever suits the person in need is the approach chosen.

The walking approach works for many reasons. Many people are more comfortable with a walk than sitting in their home for a visit. It can be less awkward for the visitors, too. This makes it especially well-suited for groups where not everyone is close. Sometimes it's easier to talk about life's big issues with them.

Be sure to remind each walker to call and confirm before meeting. Keep in mind that while grieving, it may be difficult for them to complete every walk as planned. That's okay! One group considers success to be 50 percent of the scheduled dates being walked. Don't push the griever. Let them be in control and follow their lead. If they ask to walk in silence, accept that without taking it personally. Remember: your mere presence is helpful. If they're not up to walking, offer to sit with them instead.

Clay Cockrell, a licensed clinical social worker, has taken therapy off the couch and out into nature. His counseling sessions take place during walks through New York City's Central Park. He offers several compelling reasons why walking someone through grief can be so productive.

1. Walking and talking makes the session more casual. The eye contact issue can make sitting across from each other too formal and stiff. This is just two friends walking. A more casual interaction. Also, it's a metaphor for moving forward. When we sit and talk, you're inward. It's stationary. While walking, we're breathing more deeply, we're moving. It's more dynamic.

2. Studies show that exercise helps our mental health. Endorphins are released, toxins are cleaned out, and our heart rate's a little higher. It's not strenuous exercise, but you are moving. This improves our sense of well-being, and helps to relieve depression and anxiety. Many people think better on their feet. Queen Elizabeth conducts meetings while standing!

3. This kind of activity helps mitigate the isolation we may feel while grieving. Many times this is the only time my clients get out. In New York City, we often go from apartment to subway to cubicle, so this is a wonderful time to be around other people. Particularly helpful for people in grief, is knowing that life goes on. It energizes us. Isolation keeps us back, in our heads too much. What I love about this walking calendar is it keeps people from staying away because they don't know what to say. We don't want to say the wrong thing, which isolates the person even further. This way you have

a standing date. Every Wednesday, we'll walk, or however it's set up. In my experience, the person just wants to be heard, so this is a great idea.

The Bottom Line: It's likely others are feeling the same as you: wanting to help, but unsure as to how. Help each other by working together.

Resources

- Walkandtalk.com
- Find a dove release company here: www.whitedovereleasesociety.com
- Plant a Memory Tree: www.arborday.org

Sympathy does not think. It acts.

~Sri Chinmoy

5

The Most Painful Mistake People Make

5

The Most Painful Mistake
People Make

The only thing worse than doing the wrong thing, is doing nothing.

The only thing worse than saying the wrong thing, is saying nothing.

There are a hundred reasons why we avoid people who have lost someone. We're afraid of saying something that will make them feel worse. We mistakenly believe that if we don't bring it up, they won't think about it. We don't know how to deal with such intense emotions.

The anthropologist Margaret Mead noticed this. She said, "When a person is born we rejoice, and when they're married we jubilate, but when they die we try to pretend nothing has happened." Imagine how this makes the grievers feel. They have experienced profound loss, pain beyond measure, yet many around them will act as though everything is just fine. Psychologists often cite isolation as one of the main dangers while grieving. What could be more isolating than the silence of others? No wonder some people default to social withdrawal. Who can blame them?

A woman whose husband died a few years ago told me, "Some of our closest friends have faded into the background since Steve died. I think it's too hard to face what has happened. Do they think it's contagious?" She laughed, but shook her head. "It's painful to lose your partner, then lose so many of your friends, too. I want to talk about old times, tell old jokes, but they just can't, I guess."

I have a neighbor whose wife died almost a year ago. I was shocked to hear her brother hadn't spoken to him since her death. "Not even to the kids?" I asked. "Not even on the kids' birthdays!" he said. "No visits, no phone calls, not so much as a card. It's been one of the hardest things for me to understand. I mean, why? I know he's having a hard time, but we all are. This just makes it harder. So much harder."

Lelani had a similar experience when her husband died. "My husband had two brothers who live in our same town and they decided it was just too painful, and completely disappeared. They were in the hospital room with us as he died. Right after they came over and hugged me and cried and said they would always be there for me and the kids.

Anything we needed, they would always take care of us. Well, that was the last time I saw them except for the funeral. Every once in a while, my kids talk to them on Facebook or whatever, but that's it. They got lost in their pain, I guess. It was really hard for me. I know it was hard for them, but it was hard for me, too! Their mother has stayed close, though. It's been eleven years, and we just spoke yesterday, as a matter of fact. That helps."

Claudia Church learned through personal experience how important it is to say something. "Today when I hear the news that someone is sick, struggling, or has lost a friend or family member I now reach out with phone calls and cards to help them get through their grief. I used to think I wouldn't be able to say the right words, but after witnessing the impact personal contact can truly make, I will never hesitate again. Silence from others to a grieving person says lack of caring and adds to the feelings of aloneness. The joy heard in the voice of a grieving person upon receiving a card or phone call is healing . . . very healing and truly priceless."

Bottom Line: Whatever you do, don't ignore someone's loss.

Resources

If you can't bring yourself to visit, send a card. Don't know what to say? Here's help:

- http://dying.about.com/od/thegrievingprocess/a/condolence.htm
- www.wendy.com/letterwriting/condolences.html

There are always two parties to a death; the person who dies and the survivors who are bereaved.

~Arnold Toynbee

6

It's Not About You

6

It's Not About You

When you approach someone who is grieving, remember Rule Number 1. You are there to listen. Don't burden the griever with drawn-out accounts of your own losses. In fact, don't go into it at all. Mention it and drop it. Remember your objective. You're there to listen to them, not the other way around.

Like most grief don'ts, going on and on about your own experience with death comes from good intentions. It's human nature to seek out ways to relate to others, especially during times of sadness or crisis. We want to tell our story of loss. We want to share what we've learned about grief, in the hopes of making the other's journey a bit easier. That's the reason I wrote this book. The difference is, people can pick this book up and put it down as they wish. It's not so easy when someone comes over and insists on sharing their pain . . . *in detail.*

Suzanne's brother was killed when his bicycle was struck by a car. She later told me, "I really wish people hadn't said they knew just how I felt, then proceeded to tell me their stories for a long time."

When I ask about this kind of over-sharing in interviews, people usually groan and nod. They tell me stories of people coming to comfort them, only to end up needing to be comforted themselves. A man told me how this happened to him after his wife died. "Friends came over right after Maggie died. I would barely get out how it happened and they would start telling me about someone in their family who died. We switched places, kind of. I wished I could have gotten it out more in those first days. Maybe they thought I didn't want to talk about it, but I did."

It can be difficult to hold back. It's only natural to want to tell the person who is grieving of the similarities or differences between your loss or losses. Understand, though, how that can sound to the griever. Although your aim is not to belittle their pain, that's how such a conversation can make them feel. If you delve into your situation, you will be making it about you.

In the depths of grief, most people are unable to take on anyone else's pain. When others focus on their own story, they are (unintentionally) burdening the person they have come to comfort. Jan Davies has this to say about the "walking wounded":

So many of us have had less than ideal opportunities to share our losses in a way that brings healing. Our families and culture in general often ask us to close off our grief rather than feel it in order to move through it. The busyness of work and family encourages us to ignore the needs of our grief, and may leave us in a state of denial. To be a quality support person to the bereaved, it helps when our own issues of loss have been processed, experienced, and supported. I don't need to be a trained counselor to know whether another's loss is waking up my own unresolved grief. The bereaved need our understanding and empathy, not another deep well of loss added to their own. How do you know if your own grief is getting in the way of supporting another? There is a distinct difference between remembering emotional pain and feeling emotional pain as if the loss happened yesterday. Do you feel the need to spend more time talking about your own loss rather than listening to the needs of your friend? Do you interrupt your friend's sharing in order to tell your own story? Is your bereaved friend comforting you? If you answer yes to any of these you may be one of the "walking wounded." Find a friend or counselor who can hear your story and let you feel your pain, regardless of how long it has been since the loss.

This isn't to say you should never discuss your loss with the person you are supporting. If the person asks, by all means share your experience. Learning from each other is the reason I wrote this book. After twenty-one years of marriage and five kids, DeNece Hone-Beckman lost the love of her life when her husband, Rick, died. "The stream of support that I have gotten from 'those that have grieved before me' has been invaluable to me in this journey. . . . I am so grateful for the connections that I've made, and the thoughts-feelings that have been shared. It's given me *great* comfort, and shown me that I am not alone, even when I feel *most alone.*"

The Bottom Line: Keep your story of loss to a minimum. It's about them. If they want to know more, they'll ask.

Resources

- Read Dr. Michael D. Sedler's book *When to Speak Up and When to Shut Up.*

If speaking is silver, then listening is gold.

~Turkish proverb

One friend, one person who is truly understanding, who takes the trouble to listen to us as we consider a problem, can change our whole outlook on the world.

~Dr. E. H. Mayo

7

Humor Can Be Healing

7

Humor Can Be Healing

I've found humor to be a mainstay in the recovery of most people. If you have been through a life crisis, you probably know what I mean. If not, I want you to be prepared for what you might otherwise consider to be morbid, or dark, humor among those who grieve together. It's not meant to be disrespectful in any way.

Grace Rodriguez, president of the marketing firm AYN Brand, writes:

> From the outside looking in, tragedies are no laughing matter. Lives are lost, ruined, or haunted forever. People may perceive any form of humor in

a crisis situation as a sign of callousness or insensitivity. Humor, however, has shown time and time again that it is one of our best stress mitigators; and this benefit may prove useful in a crisis situation. It helps people cope with the situation; relieves tension; provides perspective; helps people bond; and offers much-needed hope and optimism through levity. It helps people face threat and fears instead of succumb to them. For those directly affected by the crisis, it can help them shock themselves out of the horrors or anxiety of the disaster. It can also help people through any residual grieving process.

Many families rely on jokes that others might consider inappropriate, when in fact, they may be anything but.

Tanya Boyle's family had what some call a death storm, or several deaths close together. In one year's time, she lost her mother, stepfather, and grandmother. Her grandmother died shortly before Thanksgiving. None of her family members wanted to face all those empty chairs at the dinner table that year, so they planned a trip instead. Twenty of them traveled to Disneyland and checked into a beautiful hotel. As they all loaded into the hotel's shuttle to the park, Tanya announced from the front of the bus, "You've just lost half of your immediate family. What are you going to do now?" to which her family loudly answered, "We're going to Disneyland!" As they laughed and hugged each other, Tanya could only imagine what the bus driver was thinking.

Humor can be a hugely effective release. Much like crying, it can provide relief when you're too overloaded to do anything else. We say and do things while emotionally drained and sleep-deprived that are so ridiculous we have to laugh. And why not? These jokes are often sanity-savers. They can bond people in crisis, and are often remembered and repeated long after the crisis itself.

When my mother died, my sister and I were in our early 20s and completely unprepared for handling what everyone referred to as "the arrangements." One afternoon we sat by the phone, wondering how you're supposed to pick a crematory. We opened the phone book and looked at the ads. No discernible difference. I decided to call and ask for prices. Why not? We had to make a decision somehow. I picked up the phone and called the first one listed. When they answered, I said, "Hi. I, uh, we've got this body, and I wanted . . ." My sister quickly hung up the phone. I asked her what she thought she was doing! She looked at me like I was insane and slowly repeated, "We've got . . . this body?!" To this day I don't know what I was thinking, but I can't tell you how many times we have laughed at that stupid sentence. When the going gets rough in my family, you can be sure someone will get in my face and recite those infamous words.

Dark humor may be our way of coping when life spins out of control. Even when death is expected, the finality of the aftermath can seem surreal.

No matter the circumstances surrounding the death,

families can draw closer over "secrets" shared during this time. Diana Doyle's sister was killed in a car accident as their mother was privately battling cancer. Diana tells what happened at the funeral. "My mom had a wig on because she had been having chemo treatments and in the restroom at the wake she told me someone had hugged her and her wig had almost fallen off. Mom thought it was hilarious because she had kept her cancer a closely guarded secret. She said, 'Wouldn't that have given them something to talk about, Darling!' I think people need to know that laughter, jokes, etc., have to still be part of grieving, as it is an outlet, sometimes a huge emotional release."

Linda Wright's middle son was a looker. Ryan was an all-American, blue-eyed athlete. Girls had always chased him. As he entered his twenties, his mother couldn't help occasionally thinking of the beautiful grandchildren who were sure to come. That all ended when Ryan was gunned down near his home. Linda rushed to the hospital with her husband and younger son. Their oldest son, Eric, met them there. They were soon told that Ryan had died.

Eric took over and handled as much as he could for his parents. He says, "Obviously I needed to do everything possible for them. They were in no shape to be making decisions or arrangements." Organ donation was the first matter at hand. Eric met with the facilitators. Ryan was able to donate his corneas and tissue.

As Eric gently told his parents about this, Linda began to think of Ryan's, uh, "legacy." In her grief-induced stupor, she thought of all that had been lost, and the children Ryan would never have. A rummy sort of humor began to creep in. Linda says, "I just yelled, 'Eric! You know what we *really* need! Is there a way to get his . . . DNA?! Why didn't you ask about that?' We all joked about it after the fact, repeating to each other, 'Eric! Did you not get his DNA?' We still laugh about it."

These are the moments that get people through the worst times. They unite us in a way that can be difficult to appreciate until it happens to you.

The University of Nebraska at Omaha conducted a study in 1985 of death-related humor. Among their findings was the conclusion, "Death humor is seen to have functions both as a defense mechanism as well as a social lubricant; it also helps people gain some sense of control over the uncontrollable."

After Ed died, his wife and son were greeting visitors at the funeral home for the viewing. A woman walked in. They were somewhat surprised to see her, because she wasn't close to the wife, and the son hadn't seen her in more than twenty years. Still, they thanked her for coming as she approached the open casket. She looked in and said, "Don't he look good?" The family hugged her as she left. Ed's wife then turned to her son and asked, "He looks good? When's the last time that hussy saw Ed dead?" The woman's visit provided the family with a much-used catch phrase.

Even after the initial shock, families can experience this kind of bonding humor. The mother of cookbook author Emily Hoffman had a psychic send her an annual letter describing what was in store for her life in the coming year. She believed deeply in the psychic's ability to foresee her future and help guide her. Emily's mom looked forward to the letter each year. Not everyone in the family shared her enthusiasm, however. Her husband didn't buy it. Well, not long after Emily's mom died of cancer . . . you guessed it. A new letter came, giving details of what her life would involve over the next twelve months. Emily jokes that it was her mom playing a joke on them from the other side, giving her dad something to laugh about (which he did when he called the psychic to inform her of the situation).

For months after my own father died, I got sales calls for him. They were trying to sell him health insurance. Oh, the irony! I told them repeatedly that he had died, yet the calls still came. Finally, I told them, "Look, Jon has no job and no way of paying you for this insurance. Besides, trust me when I tell you, there is no way he could pass your physical." I hung up and laughed. They never called again.

Mary Solano is one of eight kids. Her mother was a sixth-grade teacher. Her father, a college professor and jazz musician. One year, three days after Christmas, her mother unexpectedly died. Everyone went home for her funeral. As they were returning to their home cities afterward, their father suddenly died as well. Both parents had now died, just eight days apart. All eight adult children returned home a second time to arrange another funeral, just days after the first. One night they all went to their parents' home after running errands separately, only to discover that each of them had brought home the same things—beer and Oreo cookies. Mary remembers the punch line: "Wow, can you tell we're all a bunch of orphans now or what?"

The Bottom Line: Humor can be the glue that holds survivors together. So go ahead. Laugh!

Resources

- *Don't Ask for the Dead Man's Golf Clubs,* by Lynn Kelly
- http://poorwidowme.blogspot.com

Those who don't know how to weep with their whole heart don't know how to laugh either.

~Golda Meir

8

Don't Impose Your Expectations on Their Grief

8

Don't Impose Your Expectations on Their Grief

Do you think your friend should be better by now? Over it, even? Do you want them to be more religious, less religious, talk more, talk less, or fit other expectations? It's fine to have these expectations. Just keep them to yourself.

There's no rule book for healing after a death. The best way to support someone through grief is to respect their process. "It's hard to concentrate. It's hard to sleep. It's hard to feel. It's even hard to breathe," says Maria Shriver, wife of Arnold Schwarzenegger, shortly after the death of her mother, Eunice Shriver. "People come up to you all the time and say, 'Take your time, it's okay to cry.' And then they turn around and say, 'Are you done yet?' They tell you it's okay to fall apart, and then in the next breath they tell you, 'You need to be strong.' It's all so incredibly confusing."

Avoid giving instructions to the bereaved unless they ask for this kind of help. Edeltraud Marquette explains, "I did not like some of the books we received, which seemed to tell us how to grieve (like the stages—it felt too stifling to me!). I did not like when someone compared the grief they felt over their eighty-year-old mother having died to me losing my not even twenty-one-year-old son."

Randy Spelling is a life coach in Los Angeles. He described something he noticed following the death of his father, famous producer Aaron Spelling. "Many people told me, 'That must have been so hard for you.' That is nice in theory, but it would be better to *ask* how that was for me instead of *telling* me how it was."

Everyone heals their own way, in their own time. Every loss is unique. Someone who has a textbook recovery after the death of one person, may react completely differently to the death of another. This is normal.

I want you to be prepared for what may happen. The griever's behavior might not be what you expect, but it's what they need to do right now. You don't have to understand or agree with it to be supportive. Simply walk beside them. Love them through it.

When in doubt, consider suggesting counseling. Professional help is a godsend for many. That said, the following behaviors are not considered by most to be cause for concern. Within the wide range of normal:

- Going to the cemetery to talk, "show" pictures, or bring gifts to the deceased
- Visiting places they frequented together
- Keeping routines that no longer make sense to you, but provide a sense of closeness to the griever
- Talking aloud to the deceased, with love, longing, regret, guilt, or even anger
- Removing their wedding ring or wearing it longer than you expect
- Keeping the room of the deceased as they last left it
- Calling the deceased's phone, just to hear their voice again
- Watching and rewatching home movies, going through photos
- Wearing clothing or jewelry that belonged to the person who died

In our society, we are programmed to act. Fix it or replace it, and do it quickly! With grief, we need to remind ourselves not to think this way. Jayna explains why: "After my son died, I had a lot of people tell me, 'You'll bounce back because you have your oldest,' or 'You'll have another one, you'll see.' Yes, yes, they were trying to help. They were trying to console me, but it only made me angrier. It made me feel like everyone was rushing me, but that's not what I needed. My baby just died! I wanted to scream and not stop. I needed to miss my little son. I needed to feel the pain of never seeing Frederick smile, or walk, or run to me. That's not something you can shove someone through."

Bottom Line: Let the bereaved grieve their own way, in their own time.

Resources

- Consider ordering some grief recovery materials as a gift. Start here: www.selfhealingexpressions.com

There is a sacredness in tears. They are not the mark of weakness, but of power. They speak of overwhelming grief and unspeakable love.

~Washington Irving

9

What Do I Say to the Kids?

9

What Do I Say to the Kids?

After a death in the family, the children are often our first concern, but the last ones we approach. Facing their shock and confusion can leave us feeling especially helpless. Most experts in this area cite honesty and reassurance as being the most important things we can give young people in mourning. The needs of children and teens can be unique, but much of the same advice for comforting adults applies here as well. Be patient and respect their needs. Let them do this their own way.

Hana Schramel was only four when her father died after being struck by a car while riding his bike. She remembers what helped most was her mother holding her close after giving her the terrible news. "We just lay there, two broken souls searching for answers. We must have laid there for a couple hours, but the closeness of it all made me feel a bit better. That's what grieving is all about. Not the tears, or the food, or the flowers. It's like you can't see past what's happened. But you can feel. And for a four-year-old who just found out her father died and didn't really know what it fully meant, it felt good to know that there was someone else who knew, really knew, what I was going through. Misery loves company. I guess I never knew how accurate that was."

Respect the griever's right to express himself however he chooses, within reason. Some kids want to talk about it, others will communicate through artwork or music. If a child wants to be outside all day, read all day, or needs all the reassurance you can muster, then honor that. Understanding and meeting their immediate needs does not mean you are enabling or spoiling them. Help them survive the initial shock, then worry about chronic behavior patterns.

A younger child is unlikely to understand death's permanence, and may ask when the person will come back. They need (and deserve) to have their questions answered in a gentle, but honest way.

Older kids may simply want someone to listen to them. Give them a safe place to talk about their feelings and their fears. Most teens will do better if you let them direct the conversation. Try using open-ended questions. This helps to get to what they want to discuss, rather than leading them where you think you should go.

When a parent dies, there is often an understandable degree of disorganization or confusion in the house. If you are in a position to help maintain the routine, this can be extremely beneficial. Consider offering to help in one of the following ways:

- Drive the child or children to school, sports, or other activities.
- Pack their favorite lunches for school, or make sure the necessary items stay stocked in their kitchen.
- Allow them to talk about the person who died.

As time goes by:

- Invite them to your house to play or hang out with your kids.
- Movie night! Let them choose.
- If you sense that the surviving parent needs a night off, arrange a sleepover at your house.
- Provide the child with opportunities to express grief through creative outlets. Take them to an art class, or a pottery painting studio. Set them up with supplies at home. Depending on their age, bring play dough and crayons, watercolors and brushes, or oils and canvas. Better yet, take them to the art

store and let them shop.

- Give them something that belonged to the person they have lost.
- Share your memories of their parent and their pre-death family.

Don't ignore what is happening, despite the child's age. They will certainly sense that something is wrong, whether they have been told yet or not. Keep that in mind when talking to them. It's crucial that you keep it simple until you find out how much they know. Imagine the shock of this second-grade teacher who learned this rule the hard way.

The father of one of my students called me at home after school. He told me his wife had succumbed to breast cancer that morning, but that Ben would still be in class the next day. After I offered my condolences, we discussed whether this was a good idea. He felt Ben would be better off at school than at home with his distraught mother-in-law. He asked that I keep a close eye on him, and to call him right away if I suspected he needed to leave. The next day, as class began, Ben asked to use the restroom. When he didn't return right away, I went to check on him. I found him sitting on the floor in the hallway with tears in his eyes. I knelt down to hug him and told him I would listen if he wanted to talk. After a few moments of silence, I told him how much

I had liked his mom, and how very sorry I was that she had died. He immediately pushed me away and stood up. Only then did I realize . . . *no one had told him.* My aide took over my class as Ben and I went to the counselor's office together to wait for his father. He explained he was upset because his grandmother had come to town last night, but he had to leave her to come to school. I still feel terribly guilty about how he found out. If I can help anyone love a child through a death, it would be to tell them to treat the child with honesty and respect. Tell them in clear language what has happened. You may think you are protecting them by saying the person "went to sleep" or avoiding it altogether, but this isn't true. It only complicates and prolongs their grief.

Respecting the wishes of their parent or caregiver is paramount. Take your cue from them. Lelani's kids were 3, 7, and 9 when her husband died unexpectedly following surgery:

There's one thing I'd want people to know, having gone through it. I was very appreciative of those who treated the kids like they were normal, happy kids. The people who knew what had happened, but they let the kids move on with their childhood and not treat them like victims. It was important to teach them bad things happen, but it's okay, life is good and we go on. We are all born and we all die. We don't get to choose when it happens, but they are not victims. It was important. I was really afraid the kids would fall into the trap of, "My dad died, what will you give me?" That was a very fine balance to teach the kids that giving is a gift, but now we give back. Every year since their father died we go to the homeless shelter and give back. We learned how to handle the grief and turn it into something good and not turn it inside and let it grow there.

Lisa was very close to her sister-in-law, Celine. Celine was married to Lisa's brother, Greg. They had a son together who was almost two when his parents were in a terrible car accident. Celine was killed immediately. Greg was taken to a nearby hospital with many injuries, including a broken neck. He found out about his wife's death by overhearing two doctors discussing it near his bed.

While Greg recovered from his injuries, Lisa cared for his son. As a toddler, he missed his mother deeply, but wasn't able to understand or articulate his situation. Lisa says, "People need to understand that with a child this age, their grief is going to come out in much different ways. Because he couldn't communicate his feelings, he would spit, kick the back of my seat in the car, and throw tantrums. I had to force him into his coat, force him into his carseat, and rock him forever to get him to sleep. I would want people to know that they're not going to be able to say, 'I am upset because I miss my mommy.' No, instead they're going to tantrum. We tried to keep him distracted in the beginning. He liked Chuck E. Cheese, so we took him there. A lot. You get a picture every time you go. I have a stack, seriously, over two inches thick from those visits!"

Be sensitive to the age and personality of the child. We may instinctively want to hug them, but if they don't respond well to this approach, respect that. Teenagers can be especially sensitive to feeling overloaded by well-meaning adults.

Country singer Michael Peterson told me, "I was at my dad's funeral dinner. I was 17 and meeting all of these folks who knew my dad, but I had never met before. Sooooo many of them told me, 'We sure do love you.' I thought this was so inappropriate since I had never met them before. It was weird for me and also hard to hold my tongue since I was already filled with my own grief. It was all I could do not to look at them and say, 'No you don't! I've never even met you.'"

A child's need for honesty only increases. The older the child, the more information he is likely to want. Although it is certainly difficult to tell them about something so painful, not telling them can be worse.

Singer Susan Ashton learned this when she was a teenager:

I met Danny Dulin when we were eleven years old. He was a cowboy. We just became best friends. He was always happy and fun to be around. When we got older and started driving, he would drive me out to the farm and we'd talk when things were hard for me. He was my best friend, but we loved each other, too. He always told me he was going to marry me. He drew up plans for the horse farm, and house and barn he was going to build for me. It sounds like a fairy tale, I know, but it was like that. We graduated from high school and he went to college and played football. Well, one day when I was nineteen, my friend Misty called me. She said, "Susan, why weren't you at the funeral today?" "What funeral?" I asked. "Danny Dulin's," she said. Well, I about passed out. I was on the 19th floor and I felt like I had just got sucked into the basement. Misty said she had called my dad the week before and told him Danny was in a car wreck and died. She had told him about the funeral, where, when, and everything, but he never told me! I felt like I was outside my body. I called my dad. You know what he said? His answer to me was he didn't tell me because he didn't want me to be upset. "Well, what do you think I am now?" I didn't get to say good-bye to him. I didn't get to see his family for the funeral. All because my dad didn't want me to be upset.

Remember the advice from the beginning of this chapter. Honesty and reassurance are key when supporting a young person through grief.

Kyle Breen is a college student. He is also a cancer survivor. His mother Donna wrote about his battle with neuroblastoma in her book, *Cancer's Gift*. After years as a camper at Camp Okizu, Kyle now serves as a counselor there each summer. This camp serves the childhood cancer community through specialized programs, including bereavement. He shares what he has learned from losing close friends as well as from his training as a counselor:

- Whether I'm talking to little kids at camp, my friends, or anyone, once the conversation turns to grief I shut up. I try and really listen. I don't want to cut them off.

- When a person needs to talk to someone about their grief and chooses you, recognize that. Just stay quiet and let them get it out. It's usually the only thing you can do, and the best thing you can do.

- Most kids will act out at some point after someone dies. They're trying to get your attention. This can manifest in a number of ways. Some kids will go off into their own little world and refuse to participate. They might act crazy or be disruptive. Teens might come off smug or just shut down. Keep in mind we are all different and come from a different place. Be patient and meet them where they are.

Camp Okizu is now a family tradition for the Breens. Kyle's sisters have attended too. Sadly, they have seen many of their friends die from cancer. The Breen kids all speak to how camp has helped them deal with these losses.

There are many bereavement camps for kids. These can be wonderful places for children of all ages to speak openly about their loss. Finding others who understand their feelings can be tremendously healing.

Comfort Zone Camp is the nation's largest camp provider for children. Their camps are offered free of charge to children ages 7 to 17 who have experienced the death of a parent, sibling, or primary caregiver. The camps are held year-round in several states across the country.

Bottom Line: Kids grieve too. Allow them to express themselves. Listen and be patient.

Resources

- www.beyondindigo.com/children
- www.aacap.org/cs/root/facts_for_families/children_and_grief
- www.comfortzonecamp.org
- www.okizu.org
- www.griefspeaks.com

Death leaves a heartache no one can heal, love leaves a memory no one can steal.

~From a headstone in Ireland

10

Write It Down!

10

Write It Down!

Have you ever been to a funeral where they invited everyone to share their memories of the deceased? When it goes well, you hear story after story, each revealing a side of the person you may not have known existed. Speakers keep their remarks brief, clear, and appropriate. Friends and family tell their heartwarming anecdotes. We laugh, we cry, and everyone goes home feeling much better. When it goes badly, however, it can go very badly indeed. Either no one comes forward, which makes everyone uncomfortable, or the storyteller rambles.

Pastors tell me of those especially memorable times when speakers tell unflattering or inappropriate stories, revealing all the wrong things about the person they are supposed to be honoring. The likely reason for this is nervousness. We've all probably heard that more people have a greater fear of public speaking than of death, right? That might explain it.

Nancy C. C. Smith tells what happened after her father died. "There was a man who (unfortunately) chose to speak at my dad's funeral, and actually blamed my dad for his own death! He shared how angry he was at him because he didn't listen to this quack's way of getting healthier—special vitamins and minerals, changing his diet. I almost got up to force him to sit down, but respected my mom too much to do so."

Many people, perhaps most, will be comfortable rolling the dice when it comes to opening up the floor during the funeral or memorial service. There is no need to offer an alternative unless you're concerned the family might not react well to an off-the-cuff comment. If you feel there's a loose cannon among the expected attendees, consider stepping in with one of the following options.

- If time permits, suggest to the family they review each speaker's remarks. A quick outline by way of e-mail does the job. This reduces the chances of a speech disaster, but it's no guarantee. Nerves can derail even the most polished eulogist.
- Invite participants to share their thoughts in writing. There are different ways to do this. One way is

a simple request printed in the bulletin at the service. Wording may vary, but it's usually something like this:

The family requests you send them your fondest memories of (the deceased). You may include specific events, characteristics, favorite music, or sayings. Anything at all that reminds you of (the deceased). These will be treasured, and assembled into books for family members. We thank you for your help.

(Then include an e-mail address, Web site, or mailing address where they can send submissions.)

- Have a box at the service with stacks of blank note cards and pens, with instructions to take a pen and a card and write down a favorite memory of the deceased. After visitors have paid their respects, they can put the card in the box. (Cards can also be placed in the pews before the service begins.) I have heard from families who did this and loved it. They were able to go home that evening, exhausted, and read the cards aloud to one another. If you feel comfortable, offer to set this up for the family. Take everything to the service, then make sure the box gets home with the family that day. It will be something they will always cherish. Be sure to leave a mailing address on small cards for those who need more time. You may also want to display a few framed photos of the deceased. Ask the family first, of course.

Writing a letter to the family is always a good idea. Condolence letters are a treasure, and have been for ages. In fact, they have long been what we do right, until recently. E-mails have all but replaced the handwritten letter. This leaves the family with nothing to pass down. E-mail messages are disposable and temporary. There is no comparison between an e-mail and a handwritten letter, which you can hold, feel, and save.

Jack Bank has written many such letters. "Sometimes I'm really strapped for what to say, how much to say, or what not to say. Other times it just flows. No matter how close you were or what kind of relationship it was, it's always hard. You just hope you can give some comfort to the person. It's never perfect. I always think of something else I should have said after I send it, but that's okay. I find it difficult, no, make that impossible, to get up and speak at a memorial. But I have no problem talking to people or writing to them. I'm the keeper of my family history, and we all communicate with each other by e-mail now. We don't print out an e-mail and save it for posterity, whereas a letter you might put in a box and keep somehow."

Letter writing may be considered a lost art, but even when it was commonplace, condolence letters were still special. Many families with few artifacts from their ancestors have a letter or two written about the passing of a relative. These were often all that subsequent generations knew about the person who had died. I was recently shown a letter written during the Civil War. A soldier's beloved captain had been killed in the Battle of Franklin, on November 30, 1864. The soldier wanted the captain's family to know what had happened. He described the captain's injuries in detail, and told them where he had been laid to rest:

> Dear Sam, he suffered much, yea intensely, but he bore it with the patience and courage of the true soldier that he was. . . . He fell gallantly leading his company in the most terrific charge that has been made since this cruel war began. . . . We bade our loved companion and leader a long farewell until we meet him, I trust in peace on the shores of the eternal world. *(Courtesy of the Carnton Plantation Archives)*

We can only guess what this letter meant to Captain Stewart's family, although the mere fact it still exists speaks to how it was treasured. You don't need to have dramatic information to share to make the same impact with the recipients. All they really want to know is that the life of their loved one mattered and will be remembered. That's something we all can do.

Bottom Line: Do this today, and send it! When else will a few sentences from you mean so much?

Resources

- Start here, and be sure to personalize it: www.sampleletterofsympathy.com
- Great book to get you started: *The Art of Condolence: What to Write, What to Say, What to Do at a Time of Loss,* by Leonard M. Zunin, M.D., and Hilary Stanton Zunin

Unable are the loved to die. For love is immortality.

~Emily Dickinson

11

Faith, Spirituality, Psychics, and Others: Respect Their Beliefs

11

Faith, Spirituality, Psychics, and Others: Respect Their Beliefs

We all react differently to the death of a loved one. Our responses vary according to personality, culture, faith, and traditions. This can be important to understand if your belief system differs from that of the person you want to help. The rituals of different faiths are rich in meaning. I encourage you to research them on your own to fully appreciate their history. For the purposes of this book, however, I'll provide you with a cursory description of what to expect from several cultures and religions.

Think of it this way. If you were traveling to an unfamiliar country on business, you would want to learn about their social etiquette, right? This is the same idea, only substituting the basics of grief etiquette instead. For instance, if you are not Jewish, then you're probably not sure what to expect when visiting a Jewish family after a loss. They are likely to be "sitting shiva," which is the term for the seven days of mourning together following burial of a relative. Degrees of observance vary, but generally speaking, you can expect the following:

- Don't knock or ring the bell. Enter silently.
- Many families don't hug or touch during this time.
- Visiting before the burial is discouraged, unless you are a close relative.
- Mirrors in the house will be covered or fogged—vanity is out of place.
- Don't bring flowers or gifts on your shiva call. Instead, if you choose to give a gift, a donation to a charity or synagogue fund is preferred.
- Don't speak first to the mourner. Let them initiate the conversation.
- The family will sit lower than usual—on the floor, a bench, or sofa with the cushions removed. This symbolizes being struck low by grief. You should sit normally during your brief visit.

Will you be visiting the home of a Hindu family in mourning?

- You shouldn't eat or drink there, if that's where the deceased died.
- The family doesn't cook on the day of the death, so friends are asked to provide food for them.

Chinese families have an interesting custom.

- They may offer you candy after a loss. Tradition dictates you should eat it quickly and throw away the wrapper before returning home, to avoid any bad luck associated with death.

Attending a Buddhist funeral?

- You will be expected to view the body. Bow slightly as you do so, as a sign of respect and appreciation for the impermanence of death.

What about a Greek Orthodox service?

- It is customary to bow in front of the casket, then kiss the cross or religious icon placed on the chest of the deceased. Like many rituals, this is easily followed by simply observing and repeating what those do who precede you.

Death in a traditional Japanese family?

- Don't send the usual New Year's cards to people

in mourning.
- Do send a "thinking of you during the cold weather" card in late January instead.

Native Americans have many different customs unique to each tribe. There can be important rules for the family to follow in order to ensure that the departed can continue his journey. It's best to ask someone from the particular tribe about these traditions.

Minda Powers-Douglas founded *Epitaphs Magazine*. She says:

> I admire the cultures that observe la Dia de los Muertos (Day of the Dead) because family members gather at the cemeteries to clean and decorate the graves of their ancestors. They honor their dead so beautifully. What a wonderful way to celebrate the people who shaped our lives! As a taphophile (lover of cemeteries), I love spending time in cemeteries. I wish the Day of the Dead was more widespread. There seems to be an invisible line many people won't cross outside a cemetery—they're scared or think that cemeteries are depressing. On the contrary, it's *much* more depressing if we turn our backs on our loved ones, our ancestors, our pioneers, and our history—and that is just what is in our cemeteries.

This discomfort prevents us from discussing cemetery-related traditions, such as regional customs regarding graveside services. They can be seen as disrespectful if we're unfamiliar with their meaning. Ronnie Ballentine explained how he learned this firsthand:

> Being raised in the South, my grandfather taught me that we pick up a handful of dirt at a burial and toss it into the grave as a show of respect. It represents having traveled down this road of life with a friend or family member and an unspoken promise to be with them all the way to the grave and give them a proper burial. Well, I learned this doesn't fly with everyone when I drove five hours to my childhood friend Jim's funeral in St. Louis. After an all-nighter with Jim's brothers and friends, we attended his funeral together. At the grave, I respectfully dropped in my boutonniere and a handful of dirt, and walked away. Well, this act found no favor with Jim's brother, who approached me at the car and yelled, "What the hell was that, throwing dirt on my brother's coffin?" I did a lot of explaining, but was never truly understood. We have never spoken again.

No matter what is practiced during a funeral or mourning period, the important thing to remember is to respect those around you. Keep in mind that however you demonstrate it, you are all there for the same reason.

Those who are grieving need support, not pressure. If your convictions don't allow you to support their beliefs, then don't bring up your convictions. I know this can be difficult, but if your objective is to help, then it's the only way. When the pain of loss brings a person to their knees, celebrate any relief they experience, whatever its source. Just as all people are different, so is their path. I tell people to welcome comfort wherever they find it. The pain of grief can be so excruciating that people often seek relief through therapies and activities they wouldn't otherwise have considered.

Junie is a devout Catholic, so naturally she turned to the church for comfort after her father died. She also looked beyond her faith for help, and found it in an unexpected place—a dance performance. "The support group I was involved with is through the hospice here. Twice a year they have memorial services. You can bring pictures of the person you have lost, if you want to. People did this dance, which I thought was very interesting. They did a modern dance that expressed what they were going through in their grief. It was beautiful, and very creative. It helped to take you out of yourself because when you're grieving you can be very involved with yourself. It was just wonderful."

Actress Susan St. James is probably best known for her starring role as Kate McArdle in the sitcom *Kate and Allie.* In 2004, tragedy struck when her husband, television producer Dick Ebersol, was in a plane crash with two of their sons, Charles and Teddy. Dick and Charles survived, but fourteen-year-old Teddy was killed. A couple of years later, Susan went to Mexico with a women's photography group. She didn't know any of them beforehand, but she tells of one who changed her life in a way she never expected. "This woman was a healer and she said, 'Let me heal you.' . . . She put her hands on my shoulder and it was like I was hit with lightning! I've never turned back. It changed my life. What happened was that all of the sudden I realized that whenever a thought of Teddy came to my mind I used to drop my shoulders and just cry. And then I realized when Teddy comes into my mind I can say, 'Teddy's here for a visit!'" She describes this experience as a turning point in her painful journey. "For me, the best moment in grieving and the thing that moved me on was I could embrace Teddy finally in a way that was, *'He's my kid.'*"

Mary Jo Alessio lost her son, Ephraim, in 2005. She was raised Catholic, but found relief outside her religious beliefs.

My son died from a massive overdose of opiates, methadone and other substances. He was only twenty-one years old. Ephraim was a kind, sensitive, and loving young boy and grew into a young man with a lot of promise at his fingertips. On the evening of his death he apparently went to a party where he was sold opiates. Sixteen hours later he was pronounced dead. People knew something was wrong but they didn't want to call the police because there were pot plants in the basement. My son could have been saved, but he was not because the girl with him was afraid to get help.

I did what I had to do to work through the grief. For me, that turned out to be several things—journaling, acupuncture, smoothies, wheat grass, and going to the gym. I found a Chinese herbalist who was just wonderful. There was no masking anything with medications.

I also went to a medium twice. I do have a religious background, but now I consider myself to be on a conscious spiritual journey. As mothers, we have a deep need to know where our children are. This medium helped me with that. It brought me a lot of comfort.

Lelani describes what made the difference in her healing after her husband's death: "After my husband died, yoga and meditation helped me stay centered and be present for the kids. It wasn't easy, but it worked out. I come from a religious family, so I understand the value of religion and prayer, but for me, I needed more than that. I needed to know what I was feeling and face it head on. Yoga and meditation helped me do that."

Ruth Ann was distraught after her daughter was killed by a drunk driver. For months, she barely left the house. It wasn't until a friend told her about a psychic counselor that she was able to regain a sense of stability. Through her phone sessions with the psychic, she grew sure of her daughter's well-being. She was convinced she was communicating with her daughter, and this gave her tremendous peace. She began to sleep more, and returned to work. Her mother-in-law felt that this activity went against her Jewish faith, however, and angrily confronted Ruth Ann about it at a family dinner. "It wasn't so much that she didn't share my opinion," Ruth Ann said. "That I could have handled. It was more that, here she saw what hope and healing this had given me. Finally, I had something to hold onto, and she just kicked it out of my hands. We got past it, obviously, but it really hurt. It's okay if you don't share a belief, just keep it to yourself."

Bottom Line: Encourage grievers to welcome comfort wherever they find it. There is no single, right way to heal.

Resources

- *Talking to Heaven: A Medium's Message of Life After Death,* by James Van Praagh
- *Healing After Loss: Daily Meditations for Working Through Grief,* by Martha Whitmore Hickman
- www.friendsdontletfriendsdie.com
- *Yoga for a Broken Heart: A Spiritual Guide to Healing from Break-up, Loss, Death or Divorce,* by Michelle Paisley

It is the will of God and Nature that these mortal bodies be laid aside, when the soul is to enter into real life; 'tis rather an embrio state, a preparation for living; a man is not completely born until he be dead: Why then should we grieve that a new child is born among the immortals?

~Benjamin Franklin

12

Grief-Induced ADD: What to Expect

12

Grief-Induced ADD: What to Expect

Okay, Grief-Induced ADD isn't a recognized medical term. I made it up. But if you've ever felt it, you know it's real. Also known as protective shock or emotional paralysis, it's that numbness commonly felt after a trauma or crisis. The griever may exhibit childlike tendencies, be in denial that the death has taken place, or be unable to focus or process information.

"That's one of the things about grief," explains Maria Shriver. "You can't even concentrate."

Grief can create zombies. Survivors may feel as though they're underwater. They may find they remember little about who has visited, details of the funeral or conversations, and so forth. For many people, the days immediately following a death can be a blur.

Try to help remind them of important dates or meetings. It's not unusual for someone to forget to pick up their prescriptions, pay their bills, or even eat. Suggest they pick someone to keep a copy of their schedule and make regular reminder calls to them. Accompany them while making arrangements and take notes for them.

One woman told how her fog lasted more than a year. She was scheduled to give a speech to a law enforcement group following her daughter's murder. She had it on the calendar, and even remembered it the morning of the event. Still, by that evening, she had forgotten all about it. "I'm a very organized person, but I needed help then. I stood people up, forgot all kinds of things. Just spaced it. Shock was a beautiful thing, though. I loved shock. Coming out of it was much harder."

One grief therapist offers this analogy: "It's like a natural injection of anesthetics." This involuntary protection offers a cushion as we begin to absorb the enormity of our suffering.

Alex Bronson writes, "My neighbor's husband died last year. There were certain things Kurt always did, like take the garbage can to the curb each week. I noticed she forgot to do this after Kurt died, so I started taking it out. I'm not sure she knows I'm doing it, but I don't care. She just misses him so much. She seems lost and disconnected sometimes. I probably do it for me more than for her. It makes me feel like I'm doing something, when in truth, there's really not much I can do for her."

Helen Fitzgerald, author of *The Mourning Handbook,* writes, "During this initial period of grief, you will feel a numbness and a disassociation with the world around you. People who are going through this often tell me that they feel as if they are watching a play in which they are but spectators."

This fog can feel even more extreme given the rush of panic that often precedes it. Kari Lindeman knows how this feels:

My grandmother was like a mother to me. We were very close, very connected. I was in college when she died suddenly of an aneurysm. My boyfriend Matt (now my husband), came to my school to tell me himself. I was pulled out of class and told to go to the Dean's office, where he was waiting. When I walked in, I could tell something was wrong. Matt took me outside to the hallway and told me she had died. I reacted physically. I became violent toward him and started screaming. I don't know what happened, but I just had a breakdown right there in the hallway. Once Matt got me to his car, I became very quiet. He kept asking me if I was okay. I felt numb. It's a good thing he was there to drive me home, because I can't imagine being on the road like that.

Psychologist Dr. Lucy Sweeney-Stolen explains Kari's reaction:

When we get the news of a death or a death is happening, we may experience a heightened state of alert. Our bodies have a way of responding to this emergency state, and often it's with an abundance of fight or flight hormones. It's involuntary. This is followed by a type of emotional and physical exhaustion. Think of a war situation and the resulting shell-shock. PTSD (Post-Traumatic Stress Disorder) is a good example. War, death (especially a sudden death), these are a challenge to us on an emotional, intellectual, and physical level. After the initial adrenaline flood, our bodies need a chance to recoup and recover. Our brains have a way of dealing with this to protect us. Concentration is off and attention span is diminished. During this process we need time to experience and adapt to the world because this person we loved is no longer in it.

Bottom Line: Reassure the grieving that this feeling is normal and will pass.

Resources

- http://thegriefblog.com

Sorrow makes us all children again—destroys all differences of intellect. The wisest know nothing.

~*Ralph Waldo Emerson*

13

There Is No Such Thing As a Perfect Funeral

13

There Is No Such Thing As a Perfect Funeral

Whether planning a memorial service, funeral, graveside ceremony, or wake, the person you're supporting may be dealing with tremendous pressure to attain perfection. If you're able, try to help the bereaved let go of those expectations as you help them through this time. No matter how meticulously you plan an end-of-life service, it will not be flawless. The good news is that it doesn't have to be.

An imperfect farewell does not mean the family didn't do a magnificent job. They will still certainly offer a beautiful good-bye to this person they so deeply loved. They will still give those in attendance the chance to learn a little more about the deceased and pay their respects. Funerals are not a pass or fail proposition. There can be beauty in the unexpected.

Remember the episode of *Friends* when Ross and Monica's grandmother Nana died? Ross fell into the open grave. I have since learned that this is more common than one might think. Many people have told me about embarrassing cemetery accidents. One woman who worked for a florist in California was pulled out of the grave just before the family's hearse came into view. Another woman slipped through the turf sheet (covering the hole) as the service began. Yet in neither case was the service ruined. It made no difference. Those assembled went on to respectfully honor the person who had died.

If accidents this big can't ruin a funeral, then we really shouldn't worry whether or not the program brochures are the right shade of green. Mishaps can be the most healing parts of a service, or at least provide some much-needed comic relief. Let me give you an example from my own family. Much as it seems like a *Saturday Night Live* sketch, this actually happened. When my great-uncle (we'll call him Bill) died, his wife Beulah planned his service with care. A devout evangelical, she believed that it was important to include certain hymns and scripture. However, when the sound system malfunctioned, Beulah's plans were threatened. Her daughter stood waiting at the altar, unable to sing the song Beulah had chosen. "I'm sorry, Mama, I don't think this will work," she said to her mother in the front pew. To this, Beulah replied over the feedback, "You will not win, Satan! We will have His word!" There was silence in the chapel. My cousin and I were to the side, scheduled to sing later in the service. We looked at each other, eyes wide, as if to say, "Am I imagining this?" Suddenly there was more feedback. Beulah then snapped to her feet, fist in the air, screaming at the top of her mighty lungs, "I *knew* you were going to try and ruin this for me! Evil will not triumph! Satan, you cannot defeat me! *You will not win!*" Her one-sided conversation with the devil went on, but so did the service. My uncle's life was honored and our family spent the rest of the day together, sharing stories about this wonderful man.

Apparently my family is not the first to sit in stunned silence during such a time. Georgette Jones told me how unsettling she found the first words spoken at the funeral for her mother, country music icon Tammy Wynette. "The preacher walked out onto the stage of the Ryman Theater and said, 'Ladies and gentlemen, Tammy Wynette has left the building.' My sister Jackie and I just looked at each other. We couldn't believe it. We shook our heads. We were so embarrassed."

There is no end to what can go wrong. A funeral director in Tennessee told me the FBI once showed up for a service she was leading. It seems a relative of the deceased was a wanted man, and they were hoping he would come so that they could capture him. (No such luck. He got away.)

A man from Nebraska told me how a funeral he was leading fell apart when tornado sirens sounded just as the graveside service began. "We're kind of used to these things here, but once we saw the funnel cloud, we had to rest the poor man in the vault rather abruptly as we all made a break for it to the chapel's basement."

This isn't to say it doesn't matter what happens at a loved one's funeral. Of course, the family wants it to go well, and to include the aspects of the person's life they hold most dear. After all, it can be very moving to listen to the deceased's favorite hymn, hear old war stories from their army buddies, or have their grandchildren give the eulogy. If a widow can reassemble her husband's old band, then by all means, have them play! But if they're like most people after a death, they are doing well to remember to brush their teeth when they wake up. (That's assuming they've gotten any sleep in the first place.)

The grieving relatives planning the service may very well be in the most vulnerable condition of their lives. Why should they take on the pressure to organize an event that would rival a State Dinner? Would they plan a formal wedding in less than a week? Of course not. No one would ask that of them now, so why should they ask it of themselves? This isn't a test to determine how much the family loves the person who has died. Encourage them to go easy on themselves and embrace the fact that whatever happens will be beautiful. There is nothing to prove.

If they have people there to help, consider delegating tasks to them. Food, music, flowers, and other arrangements can be assigned more easily than meetings with clergy or funeral directors. If leaving the house is too taxing for them right now, ask if these meetings can be held in their home. All they can do is say no, and they just might say yes!

Once you remove the expectation of perfection, they may find the activity of planning to be less stressful. It can even be a tremendous comfort to do this for the person they have lost. It doesn't have to be their final good-bye. They can take all the time they need to do that.

Bottom Line: Just say no to perfection. Reassure the grieving that whatever happens will be good enough.

Resources

- Here's a good Web site to help you with planning: www.funeralplan.com
- Another good checklist: http://dying.about.com/od/funeralsandmemorials/ht/plan_a_funeral.htm
- You can hire someone to create a slideshow from family pictures and video, or ask a friend to use a Web site like this one to do it yourselves: www.photo-to-dvd.com/dvd-photo-slideshow/funeral-slideshow.html
- Don't hesitate to ask your funeral director and clergyman for advice. Take advantage of their experience. They are there to help.
- National Funeral Directors Association (NFDA)
    telephone: 1-800-228-6332;
    Internet address: www.nfda.org

Expect the best, plan for the worst, and prepare to be surprised.

~Dennis Waitley

14

Grief Is Powerful and Unpredictable

14

Grief Is Powerful and Unpredictable

It's important for those supporting someone through grief to understand its erratic nature. The most innocent comment can cut like a knife. A smell, image, or sound of someone's voice can trigger a flood of emotion that takes the griever by surprise.

Just when a person feels she is getting hold of her grief, it can hit with frightening force. Imagine being tossed by a wave you never saw coming. Grief bursts are much like this. They come from out of nowhere, and knock you off your feet.

Soon after the death of her mother, Eunice Shriver,

Maria Shriver had this to say at the Women's Conference: "So you try, really try hard to keep the grief at bay. You push it back, and little by little you try and get control of your life again. And for a moment you feel you're on solid footing, but then all of the sudden it sneaks up and blind-sides you. A tsunami of grief that takes you back down all over again. The real truth is, I'm not fine. The real truth is that my mother's death has brought me to my knees."

By letting grievers know that "grief attacks" are normal, you can help alleviate their anxiety. These emotional sucker punches can be so intense and unexpected that they leave a person feeling especially vulnerable. The person may feel as if they're going crazy. It can help to know what's really happening.

Most people I have interviewed tell me that attacks of grief hit most often in the car. Whether it is simply the time alone, driving past places associated with the person who died, or a song on the radio, our cars often serve as cathar-sis chambers. (The shower runs a close second.)

"Grief is overwhelming when it hits. And unless you have traveled that road you can't imagine what the person is going through," explains Diana Doyle. "Grief is like a wound, it weeps from time to time. There will always be a scar. Grief never ends. It comes on at any time of the day. Any situation can trigger it. No one chooses to be sad or down. It's the effect grief and loss has on the human mind."

This is another reason why it's not helpful to tell some-one who is grieving not to dwell on it, or to try just to remember the good times. It's often out of our control. It's been said that the only way through grief is through grief. No going around it. This means we have to let them feel it, not try to save them from it. Hard as it may be to sit by and watch them suffer, it's the only way to begin to heal. It's not wallowing. It's what's necessary to move on.

Emily got married soon after her mother died of cancer. One day her husband showed her a scar he'd had for a while. Emily suggested he use cocoa butter to help it fade. One night before bed, he put some on. As soon as Emily smelled it, she started to cry. "It all came back and hit me like a ton of bricks. It was the hospital! You see, I always try and think of Mom when she was healthy and looked good, but one smell of that and it all came back. It was from the end. When she died she was jaundiced, and so sick, and all we could do was give her foot rubs with this cocoa butter. That smell put me right back there."

Letting the person know what to expect can be an important part of supporting them through their grief. No two people will have identical experiences, but there are emotions and stages that are common to grieving. It can help to know what to expect.

Janice Lockwood found some grief support notes that helped her. She now shares them with others:

Care Notes are really good. I got them at the hospice office, but you can get them online too. They offer them about everything, covers all types of loss.

I found these to be very helpful. I have brought them to people, I don't know if they want to read them but it's okay if they don't. They help them to know what to expect. The stages of grief, things like that. It's important to know they are likely to have some or all of these, so they don't think there's something wrong with them. It's good to let them know so they can prepare. That's where groups and counseling can help too, so they know what can happen. For some people, it really helps to talk about the person and their experience and see how much they all have in common. I was right there when my father died. That can be good or that can be traumatic. The support group through hospice helped me so much.

Sometimes, no amount of information can prepare us for the intensity of what is to come. In her book *Comfort,* Ann Hood writes with searing honesty about life after the death of her five-year-old daughter, Grace:

Time passes and I still am not through it. Grief isn't something you get over. You live with it. You go on with it lodged in you. Sometimes I feel like I have swallowed a pile of stones. Grief makes me heavy. It makes me slow. Even on days when I laugh a lot, or dance, or finish a project, or meet a deadline, or celebrate, or make love, it is there. Lodged deep inside of me. Time has passed and I am living a life again, back in the world. At first, though, grief made me insane. It's true. I have been there. I am the woman standing in the street on a Thanksgiving afternoon, screaming and pulling out my hair. That is my mother coming out the door, yelling my name. That is me, running from her, down the beautiful street where houses wear plaques announcing how old and important they are. That is me making that sound which is both inhuman and guttural and the most human sound a person can make: the sound of grief. My hair is coming out, not in fistfuls, but in a painful tangle, ripped from the root, from my scalp. That is me running, zigzagging, trying to escape what is inescapable: Grace is dead.

Karen Nash is the director of grief support services for Alive Hospice in Nashville. She says, "There are numerous ways and circumstances in which grief bursts can be triggered and often in unexpected settings. For example, I remember a woman whose husband loved reuben sandwiches was in the grocery one day. As she passed the sauerkraut she just burst into tears. I would want grief supporters to know this is normal. Grief bursts are immediate and sudden, but like a cloudburst, the person can generally reconstitute fairly quickly and regain a sense of composure in a reasonable amount of time."

Bottom Line: Grief isn't linear. Expect the unexpected, and remind the griever that this is normal.

Resources

- www.carenotes.com
- www.connect.legacy.com

For death is no more than a turning of us over from time to eternity.

~William Penn

No one ever told me that grief felt so like fear.

~C. S. Lewis

15

Don't Be a Grief Trumper

15

Don't Be a Grief Trumper

It's true. Some people will try and trump a griever. They'll explain how it could have been worse. If you have just lost a parent, they will tell you of someone who lost both. If your baby died, they will tell you to be grateful it wasn't twins. If your loved one suffered a long illness, they will tell you their loved one suffered more, and for a longer time.

One-upmanship. It's not just for class reunions. They may be trying to ease your pain, but it only comes off as some morbid competition that no one will win. The fact that you are reading this book tells me you are compassionate and unlikely to commit this crime. It's such a heinous offense, however, that I must include it. Time and time again I hear of thoughtless statements made to those in grief. These are among the worst:

When Renita's daughter was stillborn, her older sister didn't exactly provide the comfort Renita was hoping for. She told her, "You're lucky you can have another one. Some people can't, and at least she died before you got to know her. That would have been worse." To her credit, Renita still speaks to this sister.

Mike was separated from his wife, Cynthia, when she died from an aneurysm. Soon afterward, his former neighbor stopped him in the supermarket parking lot. Mike expected a hug and words of condolence from the elderly woman, but got this instead: "Oh, Mikey, I heard what happened. I bet you're glad you were already moving on. Can you even think how bad it would be if you were still married?" He describes his reaction, "I just looked at her. I couldn't say anything at first. I was stunned! Finally I said, 'We were still married, thank you,' and walked away. She grabbed my sleeve and tried to pull me back, but I jerked my arm away and left. I had to. I'd hate to punch an old lady in broad daylight."

Michele Neff Hernandez was widowed at thirty-five when her husband died after being hit by a car. She has since founded Soaring Spirits Foundation as a tribute to Phil and a valuable resource for others in similar situations. She tells of a grief-judging encounter:

Once I was attending a meeting about global widowhood at the United Nations building in New York City. I went to the meeting by myself, and chatted with people nearby about my organization and what we do to assist widows in the U.S. and in other countries. A woman was sitting across the table from me and she asked me how my husband died. When I told her he was hit by a car, she went on to ask how old I was at the time. After I answered that I was thirty-five, she nodded her head and was quiet for a minute. Then she said, "Well, I hope you aren't comparing your experience to the experiences of these women in India. There is obviously no comparison. These women are destitute, and well, look at you, you will obviously just get married again." I sat quietly, just looking at her and reminding myself that I was at this meeting representing my organization. After a few seconds of uncomfortable silence the woman continued, "I mean I am not saying that your husband's death wasn't a tragedy, I am just pointing out that you will get a new husband. And that you shouldn't compare yourself to the women in India." This time I responded. "Actually, the point is to compare myself to the widowed women in India. My job is to point out how much we have in common, we all grieve the loss of a man we loved. My job is also to raise the awareness of widows in the U.S. about the condition of global widowhood, because no one will better understand the need to help these destitute widows than other women who are widowed as well." She gave me a look as she was pushed away by her friend. As she walked away she said to her friend, "Well I didn't mean to insult her. Was that rude?" I get a good laugh out of the fact that it suddenly occurred to her that she may have said something horrific to me. Her friend obviously thought so!

I am always amazed at the number of people who will approach a griever with words like, "If you think this is bad, I know someone who . . ." or even, "It could have been worse . . ." Save these stories for someone else. They are completely inappropriate for sharing with someone in mourning. There is nothing comforting about this kind of competition.

Bottom Line: Grief is not a contest. Focus on the person you are supporting and don't make comparisons.

Resources

- *The Art of Losing: Poems of Grief and Healing,* by Kevin Young

We can't escape or walk away from grief; we walk through it. And walking, not running, not crawling, is the proper pace to be traveling.

~Linus Mundy

16

Complicated Losses: Circumstances like Suicide, War, Murder, the Estranged

16

Complicated Losses: Circumstances like Suicide, War, Murder, Estrangement

There are some situations that make it even harder to grieve. When the death is a suicide, a soldier killed in action, a relative from whom you were estranged, or someone who has been murdered, it can be more difficult to process the loss.

I'm not suggesting that some deaths are inherently easier (or harder) on the survivors than others, but there are complications to keep in mind. As you reach out to families mourning the types of losses covered here, be especially sensitive to the added stress they are feeling.

Suicide

It can be particularly difficult to come to terms with a loss resulting from suicide. As you support those affected by it, there are a few things to keep in mind.

- There is still some stigma attached to suicide. Be sensitive to this. The family may be hearing hurtful remarks from others who don't understand their pain.
- It may help to reassure the family they are not alone. Locate some peer groups and grief support services that specialize in suicide. Offer this information to the grievers.
- Allow them to speak candidly with you. They may be feeling unable to discuss the suicide openly with others. Be that safe place for them to express their anger, guilt, blame, confusion, or feelings of abandonment without fear of judgment.
- Grief may be prolonged by a need for answers. The ability to come to terms with the death can be compromised when these answers are lost with the person who died.

War

Military deaths can be complicated for several reasons. Friends and family are usually far away when it happens, the details may be classified (at least initially), and grievers may struggle with why their loved one died. These deaths generally occur at a much younger age than usual.

There are many sources of support within the military. Help connect the grieving family with the services they need. (See the resources listed at the end of this chapter.)

There is a camaraderie among those serving during war that is difficult to understand or explain. This bond can be a tremendous source of strength while they are together. It can also increase their vulnerability once they return home, and are separated from their core group. While serving his second deployment to Iraq, Army Specialist Kyle Short wrote about his friend's death during his first deployment.

It happened right in front of my Bradley. The Humvee looked like a Coke can that got too hot and popped. Three men were airlifted out with major injuries. The fourth was my good buddy, Nick. He was closest to the blast. There wasn't much left of him. Once we had cleared the area we returned to base. It's almost like we were numb from adrenaline rushing. Not too much was said on the way back till we got ungeared and cleaned up. Then it hit us all. I looked at the bunk that would not be filled by that person again, and I just collapsed to the ground. I was quickly joined by about six of my brothers in arms. It's like a member of the family at that point. There were no sounds, no feelings to the heat or cold of the concrete ground. We just sat there staring at the bunk with Nick's second pair of boots unlaced and just sitting there. The numbness I felt was shared by the others there with me. Nick wasn't the only one we lost. The members that didn't come home were my brothers, friends, and some of the best men that I served with. The feeling that we felt as a whole is indescribable, but every day as we roll out now, those guys are still watching our backs.

When asked about the bond soldiers develop during combat, and how that affects them when one of them is killed, Kyle said, "Put it this way. The commander didn't call their parents or significant loved ones [to notify them of the death]. We did."

Kyle has this advice for people wanting to support the families at home who have lost someone in the war. "If you know of family members or friends whose loved ones have not come home, please give them a shoulder to cry on. An ear to listen or sometimes just seeing your face helps with the healing. Let them talk about the person who died. It's the most important thing. People need that."

Murder

In the event of a murder, there are extra layers of stress unique to the situation. These can include the investigation, frustration over solving the case, fear of an unapprehended killer and retaliation, the judicial process and delays, and media attention. It's understandable for people to be curious when someone has been murdered. It's not understandable, however, to bombard the survivors with endless questions.

After church one day, Laurie Evans' ex-husband took their six-year-old daughter to his parents' house. They found the couple dead, victims of a murder-suicide. Laurie recalls how hard it was to try and hold it together for her little girl while dealing with her own pain and grief.

Wow it's been almost thirteen years and just to mention it still sends tears rolling down my face. I was feeling absolutely devastated over the tragic deaths of my precious in-laws, who I loved very much. More than anything, I needed to be held, listened to (without loads of unwanted advice), and helped with my daughter, who needed to stay in her routine with friends, school, etc. My church family and friends were wonderful and I had a grief counselor who was an answer to prayer. Their support was incredible and of course my family got me through. I didn't need lots of advice . . . just love, hugs, and sincere compassion. The circumstances freaked some people out and they kept asking me questions that I didn't know the answers to. They were curious and I was in such emotional pain . . . I couldn't believe their stupidity."

The more sensational the crime, the more aggressive the media. Jason Lewis found this to be true when he lost his beloved uncle, Jeff. Because of the way his family was treated by reporters, he has refused to comment publicly until now.

Jeff had been part of a group known as Heaven's Gate, near San Diego. On March 26, 1997, police discovered thirty-nine bodies in the house where they had lived. They were all wearing purple track suits and new Nikes. Their leader, Marshall Applewhite, had told them they needed to exit their bodies in order to survive. The timing was tied to the Hale-Bopp comet.

As Jason struggled to deal with his uncle's choices and his own grief, the late-night shows were full of jokes about the group. Jason remembers, "Within a few hours, they weren't people anymore, but these androgynous freaks in black high tops with a big Star Trek fetish." Journalists hounded the families, waiting outside their homes with cameras and mics. Jason remembers one well-known anchor in particular. She had become frustrated with their refusal to comment. She told Jeff's brother, "Well, we'll just go with what we have, then, and it's not going to be flattering to your brother." Because the family decided it was best not to give interviews, this meant they were unable to defend Jeff and the others who died.

Jason adds, "I wish people had known how smart they all were, near genius or better. I wish they'd known that the first incarnation of the Group was much more disciplined and noble, I thought. There was no sex, no drugs, no work, no family, just simple dress and food. Nothing to distract you from preparing your soul for Jesus. And this was the 70s! They called themselves monks, and really were. They would have revivals back then and turn most people away, saying, 'You're not ready for this.' What 'cult' does that?"

"I'd tell someone in a similar situation to avoid the media altogether. They're not your friend and they don't care about what you're going through. They'll turn anything you say around on you to sell newspapers. Watching just hurts. I'd give them lots of space and try not to judge. It riles me when they cram a mic in some poor person's mouth and ask, 'How'd you feel when . . . (insert tragedy)?' Really? How do you think they feel? Did they teach you to ask those questions in journalism school?"

Erin Runnion's daughter Samantha was taken and killed when she was five years old. Because of the massive news coverage, Erin was often recognized when going out in public. She recalls how this affected her and her other children. She offers this advice:

> I would want people to know that for me, it was totally okay to approach me when I was alone. But when I was with my kids, it drove me nuts. Everybody grieves differently, but for my son, there was no reason for him to be constantly reminded. It was so hard to go to the places and do the things we did before as a family. I had to muster all my strength

to go out and let my kids have a good time. These people made it very hard for us to be out in public together. They mean well, but there are unintended consequences when you come up and offer your sympathies in front of my kids. It's already so hard to do the things we did before. It challenges your normalcy. When people come up, out of love and say something right in front of my kids, it's really rough."

Estrangement

The death of someone from whom we are estranged can seem like a second death. We often grieve the loss of someone close to us when our relationship ends. Their actual death only adds a final layer of distance and separation. Those who have said their good-byes earlier, tend to have more peace about it.

Candy Cameron experienced this within her family. Her brother-in-law had been unable to accept help for many years. He was drug-induced schizophrenic and had been living in a half-way house for years. "My husband had tried to help his brother many times," Candy said, "but there's only so much you can do. When we got word he had died, it was sad of course, but not unexpected. We made what few decisions there were to make, and mostly tried to support his mother. One day the doorbell rang. It was a package delivery. I answered the door and signed for it. As I closed the door, my husband came into the room and asked, 'Who was that?' I answered, with the box in my hands, 'Well, I'm not sure, but I think it's your brother.' We stared at each other for a few seconds, silently. Then we both burst out laughing. Not in a callous way. I guess it was the absurdity. It was so different than a family death would usually be. We'd lost him such a long time ago."

The more unresolved the relationship, however, the more complicated the grief. In those cases, the death may bring up feelings of regret or helplessness over the broken relationship that will now never be fixed. Help the griever acknowledge the loss and then let it go. Eventually, forgiveness will be the greatest healer. Support them with that when they're ready.

These deaths often yield something positive. As one grief therapist describes it, "Many people are shaken after the death of someone from whom they were estranged. They evaluate their life, and their emotional connections. This becomes the catalyst for validating their current relationships in a way that strengthens them. At the same time, it helps to heal the pain of their grief."

Bottom Line: There are no extra grief points for complicated deaths, but there are special considerations. Help the grieving utilize resources designed for their specific situation.

Resources

Support for families dealing with military deaths

- www.goldstarwives.org For spouses of those killed in military action.
- www.taps.org TAPS (Tragedy Assistance Program for Survivors), provides 24/7 support and an array of programs for military families in mourning.
- www.militaryfuneralhonors.osd.mil

Support for families dealing with murder

- Contact the National Center for Victims of Crime at 1-800-FYI-CALL or www.ncvc.org/ncvc/Main. aspx
- www.spcoalition.org
- www.thejoyfulchild.org

Support for families dealing with suicide

- http://childsuicide.homestead.com
- www.suicidology.org
- Singer Judy Collins wrote *The Seven T's About Finding a Way Back* after her son Clark committed suicide.

Support for families dealing with estrangement

- *Treatment of Complicated Mourning,* by Therese A. Rando

17

It's Okay to Be Happy Again

17

It's Okay to Be Happy Again

As people move on after a loss, there is sometimes guilt involved. As you support someone through grief, that person may need your reassurance during times of celebration or personal growth. Help those moving through grief to remember that their loved one wouldn't want them to be miserable. Endless joylessness isn't proof of how much they loved the person who has died. It's no monument to the bond they shared. Difficult though it can be, moving forward while honoring the loved one's memory is the ultimate tribute. There is nothing disloyal about surviving!

After her daughter Samantha was abducted and killed, Erin Runnion experienced survivor's guilt. She shares how she copes with this, and how supporters can help:

A caregiver-friend could really help a friend in grief by providing opportunity for them to be both active and still . . . alone, but with support (e.g., taking them to a scenic place, a large park or botanical garden and then perhaps being silent with them as they explore or sit and maybe even leaving them alone while you wait at a designated location). Helping someone develop new habits—new places to go is very helpful because all of the things they did before will hurt for some time. Many feel the need to face those demons, but only the person in pain will know when and how. Options are good—after the first several months, being set up to discover new things and places helps to uplift the spirit. At that point you can expect that they will need to face their guilt; whatever the reason, however it may manifest, most people experience survivor's guilt. Remind them that their loved one would want them to find happiness again . . . and being happy is ultimately a choice.

Part of surviving is being able to look back on your relationship with the person who has died. Not just the death.

The life. Jackie Chandler is one of seven women who write for a wonderful blog called Widow's Voice. These women write about their losses with searing honesty. They take on everything from single parenting to significant milestones to finding love again. They do it with a sense of humor and a sense of hope. Here's an entry of Jackie's:

"Don't cry because it's over; smile because it happened." ~Dr. Suess

After Jeff died, I had this quotation printed in vinyl to stick above my bed to remind me just how "lucky" I am. I read it in the hard moments when the kids are in bed, the phone hasn't rung in two days, and my poor-me's are flowing. It reminds me that I'm lucky. We're lucky. Everyone of us who were touched by Jeff's existence is lucky. He wasn't "perfect." He was far from a saint. But still, thoughts and memories of him make me smile. And his ability to laugh was second to none. I got to share his life, his laughter, his love . . . and I'm lucky for it.

Donna Rankin wrote about her experience after the death of her husband. "In the past, I have often been judgmental of someone who lost their spouse, and then remarried too soon afterward. Then, when it happened to me, I was the worst offender and found myself remarried within six months! It was meant to be, because we just celebrated our sixteenth wedding anniversary. I can now understand why getting over it, moving forward, and finding someone new to give our love to and be loved by, is a very good thing."

Holocaust survivor Frances Cutler Hahn agrees. She credits love with being able to find happiness after a remarkably painful childhood. Born in Paris in 1938, she was the daughter of parents very aware of the danger posed by the Nazis. It was safer for Jewish children to be in a children's home at that time, so her parents placed her in one when she was three years old. Her mother visited daily until the staff asked her to come only once a week, because little Frances would become so distraught each time her mother left.

By 1943, the children's home was no longer safe, either. Frances says, "The Nazis were trying to get 1,000 people per convoy. When they hadn't enough, they would raid children's homes, orphanages, or hospitals to fill them. The home wrote a letter to my father, asking him to make other arrangements." Frances would then be placed on a farm with a Catholic family, along with a dozen other Jewish children. Her mother was captured by the Nazis. She was only 28. She had no chance of survival because she was pregnant. She was taken to Auschwitz and gassed immediately.

Eventually, the war ended. Her father had survived, but was badly wounded. As he was dying, he was able to arrange for his aunt in Philadelphia to bring Frances to the United States. It took nearly three years. Frances was brought to America when she was ten, then adopted two years later. Given all that had happened to her, I was surprised to hear Frances recount her story without self-pity. In fact, several things about her surprised me, and continue to inspire me:

- She was able to marry and have the family she was denied as a child. Explains Frances, "Loving another person is very healing. I met my late husband and it was wonderful."
- Motherhood came much more easily than she feared. "I wasn't sure I wanted a child. I didn't know if I would have enough love to give to a child, but we decided to have a baby. We had Cynthia. Having her was extremely healing. Through her, I reclaimed my childhood."
- She considers herself lucky. "I was very lucky. One and a half million Jewish children died. Of course I feel lucky."

"I think I'm an optimistic person," adds Frances. "Despite everything, I've kept my optimism. Having a positive attitude toward life and being able to overcome things is very helpful. Overcoming grief takes time, but it's true what they say—it really does make you stronger. Even in the midst of great pain, things can work out. A rainbow at the end. Hope."

Bottom Line: Help them move forward. Reassure them as they find happiness in their new normal.

Resources

- http://widowsvoice-sslf.blogspot.com

All things grow with time—except grief.

~Jewish Proverb

18

Be Open to Grief's Lessons and Blessings

18

Be Open to Grief's Lessons and Blessings

It's hard to imagine anything good coming from such pain, right? It might seem odd to even consider such a thing. In time, however, many people discover just that. One woman described herself as "a superficial, materialistic pig," before her young daughter died. She told me how her outlook on everything changed as she began to recover. Soon she no longer dwelled on "things." Her priorities shifted in a way she couldn't have foreseen before she lost her child. While I'm sure she'd much rather have continued in her shallow ways and kept her daughter, she was quick to share this example of how she had grown in important ways after her daughter's death.

Author Emily Hoffman says, "I like to say my mom's death is both the worst and the best thing that's ever happened to me. The worst for obvious reasons, and the best because we've established a charity in her honor to fight breast cancer and helped a lot of people. I'm doing things in my professional life I never would have attempted if she were still here."

A young father told me how he was never one to accept help before his wife died. He describes the changes he's made:

> You know, I just had to come to the point where I could admit there's only so much I can be in control of and I had to let God have room to work in those areas I can't control. I have to step back and take care of the kids and allow God to fill in the rest. And it happens. There's only so much I can do in my 24-hour day and I just need to step back and let God control what comes my way. I had to learn to relax and not worry about it. I'm still very independent, but that's one thing I've learned. Not to be so firm, and structured. I have only started asking for more help recently. My in-laws sit with the kids, or take them somewhere, and it's been great. For me and for the kids. I had to learn the hard way, but it's a good change.

I was struck by the maturity and candor of a college student who told me how her life was different because her father had died. "Some of my friends used to tell me they wished they had a dad like mine. I only got to have him for 15 years, but I realize I was lucky to have had the best dad I could ever want. His dying allowed me to have insurance money to go to college and study in Europe. He loved the Beatles. When I was in London I took a day trip to Liverpool. I took a Beatles tour. The whole time, I cried because he would have been so happy that I got to do that. It made me proud to think I got there because of him, and I know he was excited for me."

Don't expect someone who is grieving to find these blessings right away. It may take months or even years. In Eric Clapton's autobiography *Clapton,* he writes openly about his struggle with addiction. In 1991, his four-year-old son Conor died from a fall out of a forth-ninth-floor window. Clapton writes about a twelve-step meeting he attended afterward:

A woman came up to me after the meeting and said, "You've just taken away my last excuse to have a drink." I asked her what she meant. She said, "I've always had this little corner of my mind which held the excuse that, if anything were to happen to my kids, then I'd be justified in getting drunk. You've shown me that's not true." I was suddenly aware that maybe I had found a way to turn this dreadful tragedy into something positive. I really was in the position to say, "Well, if I can go through this and stay sober, then anyone can." At that moment I realized that there was no better way of honoring the memory of my son.

Bottom Line: Something good really can come from this.

Resources

- *The Blessing of a Broken Heart,* by Sherri Mandell

We acquire the strength we have overcome.

~Ralph Waldo Emerson

Only those who avoid love can avoid grief. The point is to learn from grief and remain vulnerable to love.

~John Brantner

Death takes away. That's all there is to it. But grief gives back. By experiencing it, we are not simply eroded by pain. Rather, we become larger human beings, more compassionate, more aware, more able to help others, more able to help ourselves.

~Candy Lightner

19

It's Not Over: They Still Need You

19

It's Not Over: They Still Need You

Grief has a definite beginning, but no clear end. It's not an event. It's a process. We don't recover so much as we learn to live with it.

People have asked me, "How long will this take? How long does it last?" I wish I could give them a magic number. Survive X number of days and you will be cured, but it doesn't work like that.

"Grief is an adaptive response that is not bound by time," writes Martha Tousley. "It never really ends; we don't 'get over' grief. It is something we learn to live with over time, as we gradually adjust to the physical absence of the one who has died. Grief softens and erupts less frequently as time goes on, but it can revisit us at any time, and in varying intensity, whenever we are reminded of the loss."

Most grief recovery programs last at least one year. This doesn't mean anyone expects grief to end by then. It's more about supporting people through the painful firsts without their loved one. Holidays, anniversaries, and every annual event and tradition you can imagine are suddenly different. For others, that second year is even more painful. For them, that's when the loneliness, the finality, and the permanence really set in.

After the death of his fifteen-year-old daughter, Sam Wilbanks wrote, "Folks at work were very understanding at first, but did not truly understand the depth of my grief, and the time it takes to work through things before you can be expected to contribute fully once again. After a few months they basically forgot, and I felt as though they thought I was using my grief as an 'excuse' at work. This made things very difficult."

Many people observe the death date of their loved one the same way each year. "It's my Wallow Day," explains Lorna Young. Her son Clark died from complications after a motorcycle accident seven years ago. "I call it the sadiversary. My friends know not to call me that day. They also know I appreciate it when they remember, and acknowledge it the day before or after. I know I'll never forget about Clark. It's nice when they remember too."

As time goes on, don't feel you need to bring up the person who has died every time you talk. The griever is still the same person as before the loss, in most ways. Don't ignore the death, but don't feel you need to mention it every time you speak, either. The main thing to remember is not to be afraid to say the name. Michelle Rogers Dippel talks about how the people around her were often afraid to speak her husband's name after his death:

> It's been four and a half years. I have lived 1,650 days without Daniel Dippel's voice in my ears, his hand in mine, his presence at my side. Four and a half years ago, our life was altered 100 percent. Daily life changed in ways I could never have imagined, and the "new normal" I live now was only a figment of my imagination. I remember at that time, people walked around me like I was a landmine . . . about to explode under the slightest pressure. I remember the awkwardness when they said his name—and then look my direction to see if I was going to lose it. I remember the relief they seemed to feel when they realized that I welcomed the conversation. At the time, people seemed to avoid saying his name, for fear I'd forgotten about it for a minute and they might cause me sadness by making me remember. It was a sweet consideration, but definitely wasted effort. Have you ever forgotten your spouse was dead? (other than the occasional grabbing of the

phone to call him-her with good news or a funny joke—only to be jolted by the sudden realization— I friggin hate those moments . . .) I mean really, would someone talking about him be so bad? I loved talking about him then, and I still love it now. It is comforting to me. It keeps him alive. Oddly enough, there are people in my life who are still uncomfortable, still awkward about it. Really? I mean how many years have to pass? I think it is easier for me in some ways because I deal with it every day. I wake up without him, go through my day without him, and climb alone into my bed at night. I cannot pretend he isn't gone. I have to deal with it all day every day. In some ways, I think the constant reminders that he is gone have sped up my recovery.

Support the griever in what many call their "new normal," or life after loss. If you called or met regularly before, don't stop now. Don't assume they won't want to continue annual traditions you enjoyed together in the past. Treat them normally, but with compassion. Encourage them as they move forward. Celebrate their progress with them.

Elizabeth Edwards lost her son, Wade, in a car accident when he was sixteen years old. Maria Shriver asked her, "What would you say to people who feel that they can't go on, that their heart is broken, that they don't know which way to turn? What's the positive that comes out of grieving properly?" Edwards answered, "If I . . . curl up into a little ball and become useless, what am I saying about my son's life? He would want me to live fully. It's an easy thing to say, but I know he would want me to live fully, but also I'm one of the only things he has left behind. So if I live in the way he lived—generously and honorably, then I do it as a tribute to him. So I take what he taught me and translate that into my own life and move forward that way. There's nobody that you care about that wants to see you in a little ball."

Bottom Line: Grief doesn't have an expiration date. Don't expect them to be "cured." Continue your support.

Resources

- *Traveling Through Grief: Learning to Live Again After the Death of a Loved One,* by Susan Zonnebelt-Smeenge and Robert C. De Vries

She was no longer wrestling with the grief, but could sit down with it as a lasting companion and make it a sharer in her thoughts.

~George Eliot, Middlemarch

20

20 Ideas for
Paying Tribute

20

20 Ideas for Paying Tribute

One of the most meaningful ways you can support someone after a death is to help them pay tribute to the person who has died. Tributes can be a way of honoring our loved one's work, passions, talents, or just the place they held in our hearts and lives. We share their story as we sustain their memory.

When my kids were very young, we didn't leave them very often. When we did, we chose their sitter carefully and stuck with them. One of these special people was a girl named Emily. Her little sisters were in preschool with our daughter, and we were friends with her family. It was a perfect match.

One summer day, Emily was killed in a terrible car accident. She was one of those kids everybody loved, and our community was stunned. I remember moms at the store in our small town, walking like zombies, hugging each other wordlessly. What was there to say? It made no sense. Our beautiful, talented, hilarious Emily. Gone.

Her family, while devastated, amazed us all. They somehow managed to survive. That in itself is incredible, but they did so much more. They celebrated Emily's memory in many ways. She was a gifted athlete, so they offered scholarships to girls going to sports camps. Emily's older sister wrote a moving article about her for a running magazine. Her parents honor her every time they reach out to other parents. Her father, Sam, writes, "I feel that as someone who has experienced the loss of a child, I have a responsibility to call and talk to friends or acquaintances that have experienced similar loss. For me, it is just making myself available to talk, but not 'forcing' myself on them. I like to call on the anniversary of the death to let them know that I am thinking of their lost child and them. My biggest fear is people forgetting how wonderful a person Emily was."

We will never forget Emily. Shortly after she died, we moved to another state. Her mom graciously sent us a photograph of Emily with her little sisters and my daughter. It hangs on our wall, and people often ask who is that beautiful girl? We tell them all about her.

An important way for you to support someone through

grief is to help them memorialize their loved one. Take a look at this list together. Once they make a choice, help them to see it through.

20 Ideas

1. Establish a scholarship or award in their name.
2. Donate a bench to their favorite park, golf course, school, or other place they enjoyed. Include an engraved nameplate.
3. Plant a tree or flower bulbs that will bloom every spring.
4. Name a school, park, or child after them!
5. Create a scrapbook of their life, from baby pictures to their obituary.
6. Continue their charity work.
7. Hold a butterfly release.
8. Many commit to positive personal changes in someone's honor. (They quit smoking or drinking, for example.)
9. Get a tattoo. Go alone or unite as a group.
10. Was the person a sports fan? Go cheer for their favorite team and pay for a special message to them on the Jumbotron.
11. Create an online memorial page for others to share their stories and photos.
12. Compose a song, paint, draw, or dance in their honor.

13. Hold a candlelight vigil. Include music or poetry.

14. Donate in their name to a cause they loved, or to their alma mater.

15. Have a birthday party for them and celebrate your memories together. Let guests each write a message to the deceased on a balloon filled with helium. Sing Happy Birthday and release the balloons.

16. Ask those closest to the deceased to tape or video themselves recounting favorite stories about them or moments they shared.

17. Make quilts or stuffed animals from their clothes.

18. Go to a concert they would have loved. Take others who were close to them. Sing along at the top of your lungs!

19. Books can be a beautiful tribute. Consider giving to a library or church. They often inscribe donated copies with names of the donor and person being honored.

20. Light a candle for them in a church or your home. Many do this on the person's birth date or death date.

When Pax Michael Falotico was stillborn, his parents began performing random acts of kindness in his memory. They suggest a few simple ideas for honoring someone this way:

- Pay for someone's meal or gas.
- Volunteer your time.
- Donate to a cause.
- Help an elder with yard work, shopping, or cleaning.
- Spend time with someone who is lonely.
- Cook a meal for someone.
- Pay for someone's utility bill.
- Leave an extra-large tip for your food server.
- Leave a bouquet of flowers on someone's doorstep.
- Plug someone's parking meter.
- Leave change in the vending machine for the next person.
- Buy coffee for the person standing behind you in line.
- Crochet a baby's blanket and take it to the hospital nursery.

Bottom Line: A tribute can be anything that honors that person's memory. You don't have to spend a lot of money to make a big impact.

Resources

- www.memories-are-forever.org
- www.gonetoosoon.org

The most profound way to honor someone who has died is to live, not just exist, but to try new things like skydiving or chasing your dreams. Perhaps you simply notice the glisten of morning dew on the lawn, or listen to the sound of children laughing. Take a moment to be alive, in memory of those who can't!

~*Diana Doyle*

The Stages of Grief

The Stages of Grief

Denial
Anger
Bargaining
Depression
Acceptance

Warning Signs

Warning Signs

I'm not a doctor. This section is provided as a general guide only. If you have concerns, always consult a professional.

Grief counseling and peer support groups are a tremendous resource for most people. A person doesn't need to be experiencing the kinds of problems described here to benefit from grief therapy, peer support groups, or bereavement camps.

These warning signs are meant to alert a supporter to more severe difficulties, which may require intervention to resolve.

Some people will need more than your love and support to begin to heal from their loss. For those exhibiting the following signs, suggest they seek professional help. Do this in a gentle, non-judgmental way. Find a local counselor, doctor, or treatment program and give them the number. If they're open to it, make an appointment and drive them there.

Seek help if you witness any of these behaviors (for teens, consider both lists):

- Abuse of alcohol or drugs
- Talking about suicide
- Neglecting their personal hygiene
- Psychotic states
- Irrational thinking
- Harming themselves
- Denial that the death has occurred
- Severe weight change or eating disorder
- Excessive sleeping or inability to sleep
- Violence

Seek help for children showing one or more of these signs:

- A long period of depression causing the child to retreat from activities and people they would normally enjoy
- Prolonged insomnia
- Inability or refusal to eat
- Other food control issues (single food acceptance, hiding food, etc.)
- Expressing a desire to join the person who has died (depending on age and understanding of death)
- Serious decline in grades, truancy

- Regression that persists or seems excessive (bed-wetting, thumb-sucking, etc.)
- Tantrums or anxiety that appear troubling to the caregiver

Bottom Line: Trust your gut. If you fear your friend is in need of more help, then bring it up gently. Offer them help.

Resources

- If suicide is a possibility, calling 911 is appropriate.
- So is 1-800-SUICIDE, which is staffed by counselors 24/7.
- Hospices offer aftercare for the bereaved: National Hospice and Palliative Care Organization - Telephone: 1-800-658-8898 (End-of-Life Consumer Helpline); Internet address: www.nhpco.org
- Hospice Net Internet address: www.hospicenet.org
- Griefnet: www.griefnet.org
- Parents Without Partners International, Inc. - Telephone: 1-312-644-6610; Internet address: www.parentswithoutpartners.org
- Candlelighters Childhood Cancer Foundation Telephone: 1-800-366-2223; Internet address: www.candlelighters.org

- The Compassionate Friends Telephone: 1-877-969-0010 Internet address: www.compassionatefriends.org

Listen for the "cry for help." You might be the only one that hears it.

~Kirsti A. Dyer, M.D., M.S.

10 Things You Should Never Say

10 Things You Should Never Say

How are you doing?

I can't tell you how many people have told me that this well-meaning question is especially infuriating to them. Most admit to being tempted to answer, "How the (bleep) do you think I'm doing?"

I know how you feel.

Trust me when I tell you, you don't. Every person is unique, every relationship is unique; therefore, all grief is unique. It's okay to think it, just don't say it.

The same thing happened to me.

You may have lost someone too, but you are not me, losing them. It's different.

Don't cry.

Crying is normal and healthy. Don't discourage someone from releasing their emotions this way.

It's for the best, or It's a blessing.

I shouldn't have to explain how a devastating loss should never be called a blessing.

You'll marry again, or you'll have another child, etc.

People aren't replaceable. Spouses and children are not interchangeable.

It could have been worse.

Maybe, but I fail to see how that helps right now.

Time heals.

I sure hope so, but I'll never stop missing them.

These things happen.

I know you mean well, but this trivializes my loss.

They're in a better place.

Possibly, but right now my arms are empty.

How to Help Right Now

How to Help Right Now

Has someone passed and you're on your way to see the family? Need ideas for what to do for them right this minute? No problem. Skim through the following list and get started, then read the book for a better understanding and more details.

Every situation is different. Every family is different. Take a look and offer what feels right:

Be There

- Visit.
- Call.
- Listen.
- Be their driver.
- Make calls for them (make or cancel appointments, notify family, friends, work, school, church, etc.).

Funeral or Memorial Service

- Accompany the family to the funeral home.
- Help them plan the service, then carry out arrangements.
- Assist them with the obituary.
- Set up any special features, such as:
  Music
  Memory notecards
  Photo display
  Memorial Web page
  Video of life story
  Food for wake or family gathering afterward
  Dove butterfly, or balloon release
  An order for the family's choice of flowers
- Help them write thank-you notes. Stamp and mail them.
- In some cities, many homes are burglarized during funerals. Have someone house-sit during the service, for peace of mind.

Food

- Take food for family and visitors.
- Set up dinner calendar for ongoing support.
- Find out which retailers or restaurants the family could benefit from through gift cards. Share this information with others who ask how they can help.

Organize Others

- Set up a dinner or walking calendar.

Practical Tasks

- Mow the lawn, pull weeds.
- Wash their car.
- Offer specific housework favors.
- Ask what errands you can run—dry cleaning, dog to the groomers, etc.
- Put up out-of-town guests.
- Volunteer for airport pick-ups, drop-offs.
- Walk the dog.
- Buy groceries, restock the basics.
- Drop off board games to occupy kids and visitors.

Write to Them

Write a letter of condolence, or even a few lines in a greeting card. Just be sure to include something personal. It can be what you admired about the person who has died, a joke you shared, a song that reminds you of them, and so forth. Especially healing are times the deceased told you how he loved or appreciated the person you're writing. Be sure to describe these special moments. It will mean the world to them.

Lyrics from a Song

Lyrics from a Song

I've been a songwriter for most of my life. This is a song I wrote with Candy Cameron soon after the death of my father. At the time, I thought I was just describing my journey back after losing him. In hindsight, I see it was actually the beginning of this book.

Don't Tell Me

You don't want to see me cry like this
But it's nothing you can fix
You don't want to see me in this pain
And if you could, you'd wave a wand
And bring him back again
But you can't
That's just the way it is

I know you mean well
But if you really want to help

Don't tell me
It was meant to be
Or it must have been his time
Or time is all I need
No, don't tell me
How to let him go
I promise that's the one thing I will know
Even if you don't tell me

Something in that moment when I wake
It hits me and I break
Shattered like a mirror on the floor
I see myself in every piece
I had to fall apart
To begin to put it all back again

I'll survive, I know
But you've got to let me take this slow.

Don't tell me
How much I should cry
Or how long it should take
Or how to say good-bye
No, don't tell me
How to let him go
I promise that's the one thing I will know
Even if you don't tell me.

Healing

I'll be fine someday
Grateful for the love
Stronger for the pain

> Don't tell me
> It was meant to be
> Or it must have been his time
> Or time is all I need
> No, don't tell me
> How to let him go
> I promise that's the one thing I will know
> Even if you don't tell me
> Even if you don't tell me